HOTSPOTS
TURKEY
LYCIAN COAST

**Marmaris, Fethiye, Ölüdeniz, Hisarönü,
Kalkan, Kaş, Turunç, İçmeler**

Written by Lindsay Bennett; updated by Sean Sheehan

Published by Thomas Cook Publishing
A division of Thomas Cook Tour Operations Limited.
Company registration no. 1450464 England
The Thomas Cook Business Park, Unit 9, Coningsby Road,
Peterborough PE3 8SB, United Kingdom
Email: books@thomascook.com, Tel: + 44 (0)1733 416477
www.thomascookpublishing.com

Produced by Cambridge Publishing Management Limited
Burr Elm Court, Main Street, Caldecote CB23 7NU

ISBN: 978-1-84157-863-7

First edition © 2006 Thomas Cook Publishing
This second edition © 2008
Text © Thomas Cook Publishing,
Maps © Thomas Cook Publishing/PCGraphics (UK) Limited

Series Editor: Diane Ashmore
Production/DTP: Steven Collins

Printed and bound in Spain by GraphyCems

Cover photography © Thomas Cook

CONTENTS

WHAT'S IN YOUR GUIDEBOOK?

Independent authors Impartial, up-to-date information from our travel experts who meticulously source local knowledge.

Experience Thomas Cook's 165 years in the travel industry and guidebook publishing enriches every word with expertise you can trust.

Travel know-how Contributions by thousands of staff around the globe, each one living and breathing travel.

Editors Travel-publishing professionals, pulling everything together to craft a perfect blend of words, pictures, maps and design.

You, the traveller We deliver a practical, no-nonsense approach to information, geared to how you really use it.

⬤ *The harbour at İçmeler*

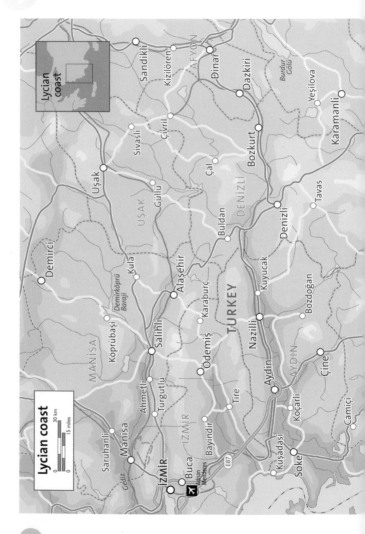

Lycian coast

Lycian coast

0   30 km
0   15 miles

Getting to know the Lycian coast

What is your idea of the perfect holiday destination? Long, hot sunny days, with beautiful sandy beaches? Crystal-clear seas and friendly people? Lots to see and do, but no rush to do anything? Then Turkey's Lycian coast – a touch of spice but with a few touches of home – is the place for you, whether you enjoy 'buzzing' nightlife or a quiet evening with just the buzzing of the cicadas.

A LAND RICH IN HISTORY
'Where East meets West' or 'the crossroads of history' – there are many ways to describe this land. The country stretches from the Aegean Sea in the west into the Middle East and Asia in the east, and it has been used as a land-bridge for hundreds of generations. Persians, Greeks, Romans, Byzantines and Ottomans all feature strongly in its long history and have left fascinating legacies for today's holidaymakers to explore.

VARIED NATURAL BEAUTY
If you're not a history buff, then Turkey has much more to offer. The sheer beauty of the landscape would be enough to draw the crowds, but here you can do more than simply gaze in awe. A fleet of boats cruises just offshore and jeep safaris navigate through forests, river beds and mountain passes. Hiking trails point the way to panoramic vistas, and you can pilot a jet-ski or kayak to explore the coastal shallows. If this all sounds too energetic, there is plenty of opportunity to bronze on the beach and dip your toes in the azure shallows with a beach bar just on the doorstep for that cooling drink, or head to a Turkish bath for a little pampering.

EVENING ENTERTAINMENT
Nightlife is varied here: the coast's larger towns offer some of the most raucous nightlife of any holiday destination in Europe – great foam parties and fishbowl cocktails – while smaller resorts are the perfect locations for romantic meals and moonlit strolls on the beach.

● *Ölüdeniz – one of the most beautiful stretches of Lycian coast*

FASCINATING COASTLINE

Lycia gets its name from the ancient people who called this region home during the 2nd and 1st century BC. Their legacy is a collection of spectacular rock-cut tombs and sentinel burial chambers that can be found all across the region, though the best are at Myra and Dalyan. This coastline is the most dramatic in Turkey.

In the east, sheer high peaks plunge directly into the sea. The region became a yachting and hippy paradise in the 1970s and remained off the beaten track until the early 1990s. It is not for nothing that this area is also known as the Turquoise Coast; the colour of the sea really is a translucent blue-green – but there's little sand for making castles.

If it's sandy beaches you're after, you need to head to the east of the region where you'll find arguably the best beaches in the country, which you'll have the pleasure of sharing with the endangered loggerhead turtle – particularly at Patara and İztuzu. The resorts in the east, Marmaris or Hisarönü, are ideal for the fun-loving crowd – great for natural beaches and nightlife. As you travel further east the resorts become smaller but with a more upmarket exclusive feel. Both Kalkan and Kaş have great restaurants and shopping, with Kaş still being the most bohemian, laid-back spot on the whole of the Turkish coast.

THE BEST OF THE LYCIAN COAST

The Lycian coast offers a wealth of fantastic experiences that fill the hours from dawn until well after dusk.

TOP 10 ATTRACTIONS

- Marvel at the ancient **Lycian tombs** of Dalyan (see page 74).

- Stroll through **Kayaköy's** deserted streets – your only companions in this old Greek village will be goats and wild birds (see page 25).

- Sunbathe on the **teardrop beach at Ölüdeniz**, one of Turkey's most beautiful stretches of sand (see page 27).

- **Paraglide** from Mount Baba or Mount Asaz for great views (see page 60).

- Take a **boat trip to Kekova**, where you can gaze down through crystal-clear waters to a sunken Roman town (see page 76).

- **Get covered in therapeutic mud** at the Ilıca mud baths (see page 75).

- Visit the wooden cafés perched over **Saklıkent Gorge** (see page 63).

- Take the scenic **coastal drive**. The road hugs the cliffs, through aromatic pine forests with fantastic views of remote coves.

- **Barter for a bargain** at a Turkish bazaar.

- Soak up the atmosphere of the **ancient remains at Xanthos**, once capital of Lycia (see page 84).

🔽 *The Turquoise Coast, Kekova Island*

SYMBOLS KEY

The following symbols are used throughout this book:

ⓐ address ☎ telephone ℱ fax ⓦ website address ⓔ email
🕓 opening times ❶ important

The following symbols are used on the maps:

𝑖	information office	○	city
✉	post office	○	large town
🛍	shopping	○	small town
✈	airport	■	POI (point of interest)
✚	hospital	═	motorway
🛡	police station	—	main road
🚌	bus station	—	minor road
🚆	railway station	—	railway
☾	mosque		

❶ numbers denote featured cafés, restaurants & evening venues

RESTAURANT CATEGORIES

The symbol after the name of each restaurant listed in this guide indicates the price of a typical three-course meal without drinks for one person:

£ under €12   ££ €12–45   £££ more than €45

◗ *The beach at Kalkan*

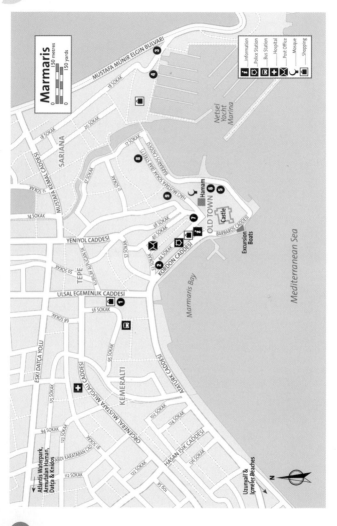

Marmaris

0 | 150 metres
0 | 150 yards

	Information
	Police Station
	Bus Station
	Hospital
	Post Office
	Mosque
	Shopping

Netsel Yacht Marina

MUSTAFA MÜNIR ELGIN BULVARI

SARIANA

MUSTAFA KEMAL CADDESI

YENIYOL CADDESI

TEPE

ULSAL EGEMENLIK CADDESI

OLD TOWN

Castle

Hamam

BARBAROS CADDESI

Excursion Boats

Marmaris Bay

Mediterranean Sea

KORDON CADDESI

KEMERALTI

ATATÜRK CADDESI

ESKI DATÇA YOLU

ORGENERAL MUSTAFA MUGLALI CADDESI

ABDI KARATABAN CAD.

HASAN IŞIK CADDESI

Atlantis Waterpark,
Armutalan Hamam,
Datça & Knidos

Uzunyalı &
Içmeler Beaches

N

Marmaris

Set in a magnificent deep bay, surrounded by rolling hills blanketed in pine forest, Marmaris has a beautiful backdrop. But it can't claim to be the prettiest town. It has developed fast in the last 15 years, and now its mainly concrete hotels and apartment blocks stretch far westwards along Uzunyalı beach. But it certainly has the biggest choice of bars, restaurants and clubs in Lycia, and a great range of things to do and see in the surrounding countryside and coast.

HISTORY

The site was originally populated by ancient Dorians. With its naturally sheltered harbour, it seemed a good place for a settlement but was ignored through the Roman and Byzantine eras. In 1522, Süleyman the Magnificent used the bay as the embarkation point for the Ottoman army that laid siege to the Knights of St John at Rhodes. While he was waiting, he built the castle and the *han* (an Ottoman guest house), planting the seeds of Marmaris' old town.

In 1798, Nelson brought the British navy here to rest before they sailed to Egypt to defeat Napoleon's navy in the Battle of the Nile. Recent years have seen a new British invasion – this time to take over the beaches and soak up the sun.

Marmaris tourist office ⓐ Marmaris Limanı (in the port) ⓣ 0252 412 1035

BEACHES

Head west to the **Uzunyalı strip** for a beach with good watersports and rides, plus hundreds of bars and restaurants. Although it is long, it's also very narrow, so people do get packed together in summer. There are good beaches at **İçmeler** and **Turunç** that can be reached on a day trip.

THINGS TO SEE & DO

Atlantis Waterpark

This water park offers numerous water slides and rubber-ring rides with names such as Kamikaze and Black Hole, plus a bowling alley, pool bar and games throughout the day.

ⓐ 212 Sokak 3, Uzunyalı ⓣ 0252 411 0462 ⓛ 08.30–18.00, later in summer (closing times vary seasonally)

Boat trips

The day trips from the harbour are excellent and take in some beautiful offshore islands. Şehir Adası (Cedar Island) is also known as **Cleopatra Island** because this is where the Egyptian queen enjoyed illicit moments with her lover, the Roman general Mark Antony, who was pushing to be Caesar. It is said that Mark Antony had the sand of the main beach imported to make it more beautiful for her. You'll be able to explore the remains of ancient Cedar, the town where they stayed.

Other routes take you along the Bozburun Peninsula to the south-west of town. There is also a regular boat-taxi to İçmeler (pronounced Ich-meller), 9 km (5½ miles) west along the peninsula. Here there is a good beach, plus a pretty old quarter to explore.

Castle

This tiny Ottoman castle, built in the late 16th century, offers great views of the old town and the bay beyond. The castle has a museum with quite a varied collection of old Ottoman and naval artefacts, but children will probably be more interested in the wild tortoises and peacocks that roam the flower-filled courtyard gardens.

ⓐ Kaleiçi ⓣ 0252 412 1459 ⓛ 08.30–12.00 & 13.00–17.30 ⓘ Admission charge

Kaleiçi (The old town)

Like a tiny pearl at the heart of Marmaris, the old town tumbles down the hill below the castle. Narrow alleyways flanked by tiny

◓ *Marmaris castle*

whitewashed cottages make it a relaxing place to browse with its small souvenir shops, a couple of art galleries and lots of traditional family homes.

Netsel Yacht Marina

The largest marina in the region, Netsel is the staging post for European flotilla groups and is also home to some of the most expensive gin palaces in the eastern Mediterranean. These are mostly owned by wealthy Turks, so shopping and dining around the marina tends to cater to their expensive needs. This is a wonderful place to stroll, especially in the early evenings.

Outdoor activities

Alternatif Turizm is a well-established company for activities including river and sea kayaking, rafting on the Dalaman River, canyoning, hiking and mountain biking.

ⓐ Çamlık Sokak 10/1 ⓣ 0252 417 2720 ⓦ www.alternatifoutdoor.com

Spas & Turkish baths

Armutalan Haamı This Turkish bath has traditional treatments, but also benefits from a sauna and Jacuzzi, combining eastern and western therapies.

ⓐ Cami Avlu Area Armutalan ⓣ 0252 417 5374 ⓛ 09.00–22.00 Apr–Oct; closed Nov–Mar

SHOPPING

Marmaris has excellent shopping in every category, and its bazaar, stocked with designer fakes, spices and Turkish crafts, is one of the largest and busiest along the coast.

For upmarket shopping, head to **Netsel marina** where you'll be able to find clothing boutiques, jewellers and craft shops.

Friday is market day, when families from the surrounding countryside bring their wares to sell. Pine honey is a local speciality.

Waterfront

Marmaris has a very attractive waterfront – *Barbaros Caddesi* – with a collection of wooden *gülets* (Turkish sailing boats) bobbing in the water and a slew of cafés and restaurants where you can enjoy an atmospheric meal or evening drink while watching the world go by.

EXCURSIONS

Datça and Knidos

The journey along the Datça peninsula west of Marmaris is spectacular, and the unsurfaced road for the final section adds to the adventure. The ancient site of Knidos sits at the peninsula's western tip and is known for its stunning sunsets. In ancient times this was a prosperous holy city, but there's little left today. The resort of Datça itself is a tiny enclave catering mainly to the yachting crowd, with a relaxed waterfront of good fish restaurants where you can enjoy a long lunch and watch the boats.

Dolmuş (minibus) services

These go to **Turunç** (see page 53) and **İçmeler** (see page 56), plus a bus service to **Dalyan** (see page 74) takes one hour.

The Blue Voyage

In the 1920s, Cevat Şakir Kabaağaçlı, Turkish writer and native of Bodrum, wrote *Mavi Yolculuk (Blue Voyage)* about a simple *gület* journey from Bodrum in the Aegean around the Lycian coast to the south, stopping at Marmaris. It captured the imagination of a generation of Turks.
The Blue Voyage takes several days and lets you follow in Kabaağaçlı's footsteps. ⓦ www.bluevoyage.com

TAKING A BREAK

Adresim £ ❶ On a busy street but good-value lunches that include salads, pizzas and Turkish favourites. ⓐ Next to the Tanas Shopping Centre, Ulusal Egemenik Caddesi ❶ 0252 413 2001 ❶ 09.00–22.00

Hemşin £ ❷ Cakes, milkshakes, pizzas, sandwiches. Outdoor tables in the shade. ⓐ Kordon Caddesi ☎ 0252 412 5793 🕓 08.00–02.00

Pineapple ££ ❸ High-quality, modern bistro-style restaurant with international dishes and an English pub upstairs. ⓐ Netsel Shopping Centre, Netsel Marina ☎ 0252 412 0976 🕓 08.00–02.00

Antique Restaurant £££ ❹ Mediterranean cuisine in a modern, refined, European-style restaurant overlooking the yachts. ⓐ Netsel Marina ☎ 0252 413 2955 🕓 11.00–16.00 & 18.00–24.00

Fellini £££ ❺ The best Italian food in Marmaris and a good location for people-watching on the seafront promenade. ⓐ Barbaros Caddesi 61 ☎ 0252 413 0826 🕓 11.00–24.00

AFTER DARK

Nightlife is concentrated along the Uzunyalı waterfront and in the town along Hacı Mustafa Sokak (known as Bar Street).

Bar Panorama ❻ Great views from the top of the old town. Limited space if busy. ⓐ Eski Camii Sokak ☎ 0252 413 4835 🕓 11.00–01.00

Cocktails ❼ You'll also see Leidseplein, Sultan and the English Pub lit up alongside in neon but they are all one and serve the same drinks. ⓐ Eski Çarşi 39 ☎ 0252 412 5206 🕓 10.00–02.30

Crazy Daisy Bar and Nightclub ❽ Dancing, foam parties and live music. ⓐ Hacı Mustafa Sokak 121 ☎ 0252 412 4856 🌐 www.crazydaisybar.com

Green House ❾ Probably the oldest bar in town, with loud music and a great atmosphere. ⓐ Hacı Mustafa Sokak ☎ 0252 412 5071

Fethiye

Nestling into a rocky outcrop at the southern end of a wide bay, Fethiye is the main port of Lycia. The town has no beaches, but people are drawn here because it's a good base for lots of things to see and do.

The town has a picturesque bazaar – more like a Greek agora with its shady vine canopy – offering a good range of shopping opportunities, some atmospheric outdoor dining and lots of boat and land tours.

By day, Fethiye acts as a magnet to the surrounding holiday resorts of **Ölüdeniz, Hisarönü** and the satellite beach area of **Çalış** (Chalush). The streets are bustling, but it's a very Turkish town, so the atmosphere is more laid-back than some of the other large holiday spots on the Turkish coast. As evening falls, it is relatively quiet – for nightlife, head back to the resorts.

Fethiye tourist office ❷ İskele Meydanı (by the marina)
❶ 0252 614 1527

HISTORY
Fethiye was originally ancient Telmessos, founded in about 400 BC. The site has been occupied continuously since then – due to fishing and its busy port. The town was called Makri until its predominantly Greek Orthodox population emigrated to Greece in the 1920s, when it was renamed Fethiye in honour of a local war hero. Sadly, few old buildings remain because of a devastating earthquake in 1957.

BEACHES

Almost a resort in its own right, **Çalış** is the major beach area for Fethiye and is only a short 5-km (3-mile) dolmuş or water taxi ride north of the town. Most of Fethiye's hotels lie along this strip, and there is a good range of holiday fun, from watersports to hotels, restaurants, bars and budget souvenir shops.

If you tire of the beach and town life, head to the freshwater marshes just inland. They are great for birdwatching and a haven for

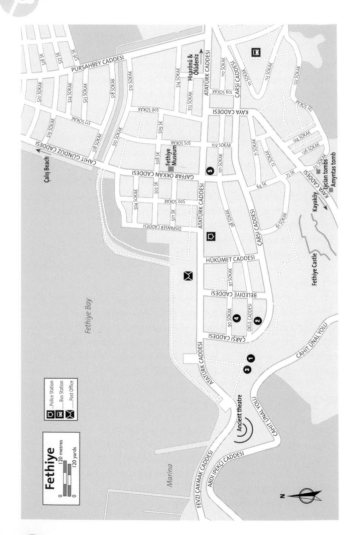

Fethiye

Police Station
Bus Station
Post Office

0 — 120 metres
0 — 120 yards

Çalış Beach

Fethiye Bay

Marina

Ancient theatre

Fethiye Museum

Hisarönü & Ölüdeniz

Kayaköy

Fethiye Castle

Lycian tombs
Amyntas tomb

PURSAHBEY CADDESI
ATATÜRK CADDESI
CARŞI CADDESI
KAYA CADDESI
CAHİT GÜNDÜZ CADDESI
GAFFAR OKKAN CADDESI
DİSPANSER CADDESI
HÜKÜMET CADDESI
BELEDİYE CADDESI
CARŞI CADDESI
ATATÜRK CADDESI
FEVZİ ÇAKMAK CADDESI
ABDİ İPEKÇİ CADDESI
CAHİT ÜNAL YOLU
OKUL CADDESI
CARŞI CADDESI

reptiles, amphibians and other wildlife – though they are also a good breeding ground for mosquitoes, so it would be wise to put on some insect repellent before you go!

The pretty beach at the small resort town of **Ölüdeniz** (see page 27) is a little further away in the opposite direction.

THINGS TO SEE & DO

Amyntas tomb

Amyntas tomb is one of the largest and most beautiful along the Turquoise coast. Photographs of it feature in most tourist brochures. Carved into a sheer rock face above the town around 350 BC, it has an impressive yet simple façade of finely carved Ionic columns, rather like a Greek temple. The inside is empty.

ⓐ Off Kaya Caddesi ⓛ 08.30–sunset ❶ Admission charge

Ancient theatre

A tiny venue by the harbour, this Hellenistic structure was updated by the Romans. It was excavated in the 1940s.

ⓐ Liman Caddesi ⓛ 24 hours ❶ Admission free

SHOPPING

Fethiye has some good shopping, and the main souvenir bazaar around the **Hamam Sokak** in the heart of town is a wonderful mixture of cheap market stalls and top-quality, fully air-conditioned fur and leather shops, where you can buy a jacket off the peg or have one made in a few days.

A daily market at **Çarşi Caddesi** sells fake designer gear and food items, and a lively market is held on Tuesdays along the canal flanking **Atatürk Caddesi**, where local farmers bring their goods.

Boat trips

The **12-Island Boat Trip** is a must. These pine-clad islands, scattered like emeralds out across the blue velvet waters of the Gulf of Fethiye, offer some of the prettiest vistas in southern Turkey. St Nicholas Island – where the saint came to worship, and lived for many years – is a popular stop (see Myra, page 82), with its remains of an early Byzantine basilica and other 4th-century AD buildings. Most boats also stop at Şövalye for its restaurant, at Gemile for its ancient ruins and at Göçek. You can also find trips along the coast to places such as Kalkan or Patara.

Castle

Built by the Knights of St John, this small Crusader fortress – only one sturdy tower remains – was built on top of part of ancient Telmessos. It now stands above the modern town and there are good views across the bay.

◢ Lycian tombs near Fethiye

Diving

Most scuba-diving companies have bases at Çalış or Ölüdeniz, and the **Diver's Delight** has a good reputation. ⓐ Bubataşı Mah ① 0252 612 6261

Fethiye Museum

The museum has a small collection of carved stone and statuary from sites around the region. The most important item is a *stele* (inscribed stone panel) from Letoön (see page 79) with words in three languages. This allowed archaeologists to decipher the Lycian language by translating the ancient Greek section next to it. There's also an ethnographic gallery with Ottoman artefacts.

ⓐ Sokak 505, Atatürk Caddesi ● Tues–Sun 08.00–17.00; closed Mon
❶ Admission charge

Lycian tombs

The most obvious remains are a series of Lycian tombs carved into the crag above the town.

Spas & Turkish baths

Ece Saray Marina and Resort A full spa with facilities featuring hydrotherapy, inhalation therapies, massage, detox and other body wraps, stone therapy, reflexology and beauty facials.

ⓐ Ece Sarayı, Karagözler Mevkii ① 0252 612 5005 Ⓦ www.ecesaray.net
Turkish bath Enjoy a cleansing massage and steam session here.
ⓐ Hamam Sokak 2 ① 0252 614 9318 ● 07.00–24.00 year round

EXCURSIONS
Kayaköy

Kayaköy was a thriving Greek village called Levissi until the founding of the Turkish Republic in the 1920s. When the Greek and Turkish governments decided to transfer their minority populations (Greeks born in Turkey were to move to Greece, and Turks born in Greece were to move to Turkey), the people of the village moved *en masse*, and Levissi became a ghost village, the largest of its kind in Turkey.

A handful of houses have been bought and restored by Europeans, and a selection of cafés and tourist shops has sprung up along the roadside at the base of the town, but much of the village is now protected. Climb higher along the cobbled alleyways and you can still leave the modern world behind. Over 2,000 homes still stand empty and the village – founded in medieval times – is a fascinating place to explore. The **Church of Panagia Pyrgiotissa** still has its frescoes and kohla'ki patterned pebble floors.

TAKING A BREAK

Cozy £–££ ❶ A vast menu, from an English breakfast to Mexican classics. ⓐ Karagözler Sokak 45 ❶ 0252 612 4141 ❶ 10.00–01.00

Meğri £££ ❷ In the heart of the bazaar, this established restaurant has a good reputation with locals. The fish is delicious, as are grilled meats, kebabs and other Turkish dishes. It also has a cheaper, less formal eatery at Çarşı Caddesi. ⓐ Lika Sokak 8–9 ❶ 0252 614 4045/6 ❶ 11.00–24.00

AFTER DARK

Barcı Bar ❸ Stay on the ground floor for that Ottoman experience and cushions galore. ⓐ Karagözler Sokak ❶ 0252 614 1340 ❶ 10.00–04.00

Ottoman Bar ❹ An interesting but successful mixture of Turkish pub and international disco bar, where you can spend time on the dance floor or relax on the low carpet-covered couches with a *nargile* (hubble-bubble pipe). ⓐ Karagözler Sokak ❶ 0252 612 1148 ❶ 11.00–03.00

Yes Bar ❺ A good place for an early evening drink or late-night dancing. ⓐ Cumhuriyet Caddesi 9 ❶ 0252 614 4239 ❶ 11.00–03.00

Ölüdeniz

One of the most photographed beaches in the world, Ölüdeniz is a golden, teardrop-shaped stretch of shingle protecting a tranquil lagoon surrounded by fragrant pine-clad peaks. The name Ölüdeniz means 'dead sea' in Turkish and is derived from the dark, motionless waters of the lagoon that have no waves at all. The landscape and coastline are definitely spectacular, with shallow, azure waters tempting you in – but there is more on offer than just the views.

In many ways, Ölüdeniz is the perfect holiday resort, with something for everyone. It's not too big, yet has a good selection of restaurants, bars and shops to enjoy. It has a beach with waves and just about every activity on the menu for watersports lovers, plus the lagoon's calm water is perfect for children and novice swimmers to splash about, and enjoy a number of non-motorised watersports.

Ölüdeniz is close to a host of places to see and things to do. Nearby **Fethiye** (see page 21) is an atmospheric town with a genuine Turkish character, while **Hisarönü**, only a couple of minutes away by regular dolmuş, is great for partying the night away.

HISTORY

Just 30 years ago, Ölüdeniz was a secret hideaway with ultra-clear waters, hidden from the rest of the world by the surrounding mountains. It started life as a hippy and backpacker haunt, with a few beach huts and tree houses to stay in, but as the 1980s progressed and the road from Fethiye was completed, more and more modern hotels were built in the valley behind the beach and the town developed into a busy resort.

Nowadays the hippies have disappeared and Ölüdeniz is a protected area, but the modern development means you get the best of both worlds – a small but lively resort combined with the magical landscapes that make this part of Turkey unique.

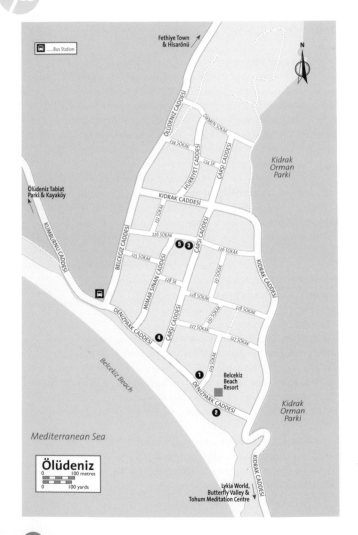

Fethiye Town
& Hisarönü

N

Bus Station

ÖLÜDENIZ CADDESI

DIRMEN SOKAK

Kidrak
Orman
Parki

234 SOKAK

234 SK.

HÜRRIYET CADDESI

ÇARŞI CADDESI

Ölüdeniz Tabiat
Parki & Kayaköy

KIDRAK CADDESI

BELCEGIZ CADDESI

332 SOKAK

226 SOKAK

ÇARŞI CADDESI

❺ ❸
226 SOKAK

KUMBURNU CADDESI

225 SOKAK

MIMAR SINAN CADDESI

228 SK.

331 SOKAK

KIDRAK CADDESI

228 SOKAK

228 SOKAK

DENIZPARK CADDESI

ÇARŞI CADDESI

227 SOKAK

332 SOKAK

227 SOKAK

❹

Belcekiz Beach

❶

229 SOKAK

Belcekiz
Beach
Resort

Mediterranean Sea

DENIZPARK CADDESI

❷

Kidrak
Orman
Parki

Ölüdeniz

0   100 metres
0   100 yards

KIDRAK CADDESI

Lykia World,
Butterfly Valley &
Tohum Meditation Centre

BEACHES

The pebbly **Belcekiz beach**, just east of the Ölüdeniz lagoon and in front of the hotel strip, offers an unrivalled selection of watersports – water-skiing, windsurfing, parasailing and inflatable banana boats. It is also the landing point for the paragliders, so they 'drop in' regularly throughout the day. Along the waterfront is a good range of cafés and bars for refreshment and sustenance.

The western tip and the lagoon itself concentrate on more sedate pursuits – snorkelling, kayaks and pedaloes – to protect the delicate environment of the lagoon. You can rent these from the concession within the national park. This is also the best spot for quiet sunbathing, away from noisy jet-skis and motor boats. The finest sandy beaches are around the inner lagoon, though none of them is very big. Most have been taken over by bars or *pensiyons* who may charge you a fee to enter.

THINGS TO SEE & DO

Boat trips
Daily trips around the bay take in Gemile beach for swimming and the Blue Cave, with a stop at Butterfly Valley (see page 31).

Diving
DiveMed Diving Centre This company runs competent training and guided diving programmes.
ⓐ Belcekiz Beach ⓣ 0252 617 0592 ⓦ www.meddiving.com

Kıdrak Orman Parkı
This natural area, just east of Ölüdeniz, marks the end of the resort and offers some shady places for a picnic or relaxing afternoon away from the hubbub.

Ölüdeniz Tabiat Parkı

The small national park, which protects the teardrop section of the Ölüdeniz lagoon from development, has a couple of basic cafés and some sports-rental stands for kayaks and pedaloes, plus shady areas for picnicking. You don't need to pay an entry fee if you enter the park along the beach.

Spas & Turkish baths

Belcekız Beach Resort Discover the *hamam* experience at this slightly touristy Turkish bath.

ⓐ At the hotel on the seafront ⓣ 0252 617 0077

ⓦ www.belcekiz.com

Seawater therapy and total wellness/fitness centre This state-of-the-art thalassotherapy centre offers various body treatments from lymph drainage and algae body wraps to reflexology, massage, facials and body peels, plus a sauna and Turkish bath.

ⓐ Lykia World Resort, PK 102 Ölüdeniz ⓣ 0252 617 0200

ⓦ www.lykiaworld.com

Tohum Meditation Centre For a truly holistic experience, visitors can come here for a week or two of peace and quiet away from the world, with organic meals and daily meditation and massage treatments. Alternatively, you can book by the session. The centre offers classes such as yoga and tai chi for beginners.

ⓐ White Cape, Ölüdeniz, in the hills above Butterfly Valley

ⓣ 0252 330 5262 ⓦ www.tohum.com

SHOPPING

The Ölüdeniz resort has a range of shopping along the tangle of streets behind the waterfront, but most of what's on offer is mass-produced run-of-the-mill stuff. For better shopping, head to Fethiye (see page 21).

⬥ *The beautiful teardrop-shaped beach at Ölüdeniz*

EXCURSIONS
Butterfly Valley

The floor of this 350-m (1,150-ft) deep canyon, which lies at the base of **Baba Dağı**, is the perfect environment for butterflies and moths. There are over 70 species that can be seen here, including the rare Tiger Butterfly (*Euplagia quadripunctaria*), in a verdant natural landscape. The 10-hectare (25-acre) park is a delightful place to explore, with a magnificent 60-m (200-ft) waterfall at its landward limit into the gorge. This area has been cultivated for many centuries.

There is a minibus transfer from Ölüdeniz to the park throughout the day, or three boat trips a day.

ⓐ 10 km (6 miles) east of Ölüdeniz – can only be reached by boat
ⓘ 0533 212 2362 ❶ Admission charge

Fethiye

The nearby town of Fethiye (see page 21) offers authentic Turkish flavour.

Kayaköy

There is a wonderful walk to Kayaköy (see page 25) on the marked path that leads up into the hills from behind the Ölüdeniz lagoon. Take water for the journey, but you'll find cafés once you get to Kayaköy.

TAKING A BREAK

Buzz Bar & Grill £ ❶ This place, which is also an Internet café, has been open forever and everyone comes here for drinks, snacks and meals throughout the day. The food is good and evenings are really lively, helped by perhaps the best cocktails in town. ⓐ Deniz Plajı
ⓣ 0252 617 0450 ⓛ 08.00–02.00

Kumsal Pide £ ❷ The oldest pizza restaurant in Ölüdeniz and holding its own; the most authentic place to eat. ⓐ Hamkamp Sokak
ⓣ 0252 617 1289 ⓛ 09.00–22.00

Sultan Peper ££ ❸ Good tourist eatery with the usual range of Turkish meals, plus a long menu of continental dishes, like pizzas, and a nightly Indian buffet for curry, bhaji and samosa fanatics. If everyone in the family fancies something different, this is the place to be.
ⓐ 2 Sokak ⓛ 08.00–01.00

AFTER DARK

Help Beach Bar ❹ This is a lively bar and one that has been open for a number of seasons. Great (loud) music and always a buzzing atmosphere. ⓐ Hamkamp Sokak (by the beach) ⓣ 0252 617 0498
ⓛ 08.00–03.00

Tequila Cocktail Bar ❺ The music at Tequila ranges from the 1960s and 1970s through to classic rock, jazz and blues, so there should be something to please everyone. As the name suggests, they serve a mean cocktail. ⓐ 1 Sokak ⓛ 11.00–03.00

Hisarönü

It seems odd that one of Turkey's most successful resorts isn't by the sea. But when you get here, you realise why it is so popular – the place is buzzing after dark, with some of the best entertainment and nightlife along the coast, and during the day there is a great choice of things to see and do within easy reach.

Every day the town empties as people head the couple of kilometres south to the great beaches at **Ölüdeniz** (see page 27), with their fantastic range of watersports. Alternatively, many visitors take the 15-minute dolmuş ride into Fethiye for great Turkish atmosphere and fantastic shopping.

There's a raft of excursions and some exhilarating sports right on the doorstep (from microlighting to swimming with dolphins, see pages 60–61), offering all the ingredients for a young, fun holiday in the sun.

Hisarönü sits in the hills high above Ölüdeniz and Fethiye, so it is often cooler than the coastal resorts. In summer, people say it is much easier to sleep here because the air is fresher, but early or late in the season (April–May and October) you may need a sweater if you wish to dine outside under the stars.

HISTORY

When the government became concerned about tourist development at Ölüdeniz, builders looked for another location, and Hisarönü, just up the hill, hit the jackpot. Most of the resort is newly built, but you'll still find one or two reminders of the farming village that used to be here before package tourism arrived.

THINGS TO SEE & DO

When you stay at Hisarönü you can enjoy all the activities and sites of **Ölüdeniz** (see page 27) and **Fethiye** (see page 21), and there are regular, local dolmuş services to both places.

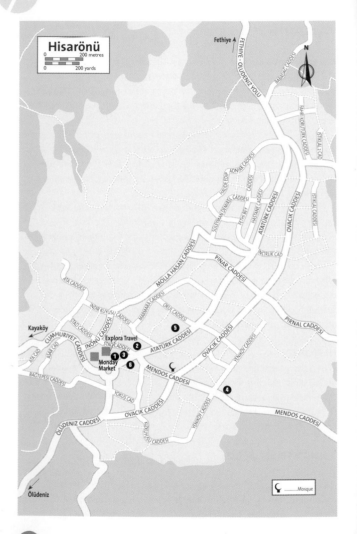

TAKING A BREAK

Domino's ££ ❶ This restaurant has been open for well over a decade and still serves good international food. The menu includes English, Italian and, of course, Turkish dishes, so you should find something to suit you. There's a lovely fire in the dining room for chilly spring or autumn evenings. ⓐ Cumhuriyet Caddesi ⓣ 0252 616 6985 ⓛ 11.00–01.00

Lemon Tree ££ ❷ In the middle of the main drag, the Turkish set menu is good value. There are also plenty of English favourites on the menu. ⓐ Atatürk Caddesi ⓣ 0252 616 6507 ⓛ 09.00–01.00

The Olive Tree Restaurant and Bar ££ ❸ One of the prettiest and most relaxing places to eat in the resort, the Olive Tree offers some really good Turkish food and a range of European dishes with vegetarian options. The restaurant has built up a good reputation since it opened in the mid-1990s. ⓐ Cumhuriyet Caddesi ⓣ 0252 616 6361 ⓛ 08.30–16.00 & 18.00–24.00

Dragonaro £££ ❹ The best Chinese restaurant in town – great if you fancy a change from Turkish or English food. It is always on the list of the best restaurants, and serves a full range of authentic dishes, including a vegetarian section on the menu. You'll need to book because it's usually crowded. ⓐ Just off the Kayaköy Road ⓣ 0252 616 7757 ⓛ 08.00–24.00

TRIPS AND ACTIVITIES
Whether it is a trip to Ephesus, quad-biking, paragliding, boat trips or a sunset cruise, compare the prices and service with Explora on Atatürk Caddesi. ⓣ 0252 616 6876 ⓦ www.exploraturkey.com

AFTER DARK

The Fez Café and Cocktail Bar ❺ A popular Hisarönü meeting place, the Fez has a good beer garden and serves English pub grub. There is even a weekly pub quiz every Thursday. The bar also has widescreen TVs for those unmissable Premier League matches. ⓐ Off Cumhuriyet Caddesi on the Kayaköy Road ⓣ 0252 616 6297 ⓛ 11.00–05.00

Zombie Bar ❻ This is a great cocktail and dance bar with a wide range of music, from hip hop to R&B. There are also widescreen TVs showing football and TV favourites. It's always lively in the evenings. ⓐ Cumhuriyet Caddesi 40 ⓣ 0252 616 6080 ⓛ 11.00–05.00

🔺 Just 15 minutes from Hisarönü, Fethiye offers the finest shopping in the area

Kalkan

Cascading down a steep hillside to its pretty port and yachting marina, Kalkan is one of the most anticipated anchorages of the famed 'Blue Cruise'. This upmarket pit stop also offers high-class dining and shopping for the jet-set sailors who step ashore throughout the summer.

The cobbled lanes at the heart of town, with their converted, late 19th-century mansions, offer an atmospheric place for an evening stroll or perhaps a bit of bargaining over that must-have souvenir.

Kalkan came late to package tourism, but it has been catching up fast, particularly amongst those who want something a little more genteel than the high-energy destinations such as **Hisarönü** (see page 33) or **Marmaris** (see page 15). In the last ten years the resort has expanded rapidly out across the surrounding hillsides, but it hasn't overwhelmed the laid-back ambiance of the old village or the jaunty nautical atmosphere of the harbour side.

HISTORY

Kalkan doesn't have a very long history. The name means 'quay' or 'jetty' in Turkish, and traders from Kastellorizo (see page 49) established a marketplace here (the only decent harbour between Fethiye and Kaş) approximately 200 years ago.

By the late 19th century, Kalkan was an important port for the goods brought from the Patara and Elmalı plains (see pages 50 and 87). The fresh produce, olive oil and grain loaded here made its way to Ottoman ports all around the eastern Mediterranean.

The town continued to thrive in the early years of the Turkish Republic but began to lose importance in the 1950s as transport links were modernised. The first Lycian coastal road was completed in the early 1960s, so the port was no longer needed and most of the population moved away. At around the same time, the first tourists arrived – intrepid, wealthy foreigners sailing their yachts into the harbour, while bohemian Turks (including one of Turkey's first rock stars)

◗ *The atmospheric seaside town of Kalkan boasts Lycia's prettiest harbour*

began to renovate the old houses as *pansiyons*, which introduced the Turkish upper classes to the resort.

Once the road from Kalkan to Fethiye was sealed in 1984 and Dalaman airport opened, the resort began to open up to package tours.

BEACHES

Kalkan is not renowned for its beaches. Most swimming takes place in concrete lidos or directly from the rocks. **İbo** is a small sandy beach to the left of the harbour, and there's another shingle stretch a few

minutes' walk south of the resort centre. The best by far is at **Kaputaş**,
7 km (4 miles) east at the mouth of the gorge. Kaputaş beach has a
spectacular setting but there are no watersports and few amenities,
so you will need to take provisions.

THINGS TO SEE & DO

Canoeing
Enjoy a day kayaking around Patara National Park and the Xanthos
River with qualified and insured guides. **Abi Travel** also arranges
other excursions to surrounding attractions.
ⓐ Yalı Bolu Mah 8 ❶ 0242 844 2694 Ⓦ www.abitravel.net

Diving
Take training towards dive qualifications or simply do an accompanied
dive to discover the sport. There are a couple of wrecks just offshore,
including the 19th-century *Duchess of York*, built in Hull. **Dolphin Scuba
Team** (❶ 0242 844 2242) and **Barracuda Dive Centre** (❶ 0242 844 3955
Ⓦ www.dive-turkey.com) are both in Kalkan harbour and have qualified
instructors and dive guides.

Watersports
Blue Marlin watersports A range of activities including sailing, jet-skiing,
windsurfing and fishing from the harbour area.
ⓐ Hotel Pirat, Kalkan Harbour ❶ 0242 844 2849

EXCURSIONS
Bezirgan
This large farming community set on a verdant plain used to be the
summer grazing and farming lands of the inhabitants of Kalkan, and
much of the population would live here. It is still a vibrant place and
provides an interesting contrast to the chic lifestyle of the coastal resort.
ⓐ About 17 km (10½ miles) inland from Kalkan

Owlsland

Erol and Pauline, a Turkish/Scottish couple, have renovated Erol's traditional family farm and now offer accommodation, meals and full-day guided walking tours of Bezirgan, taking in the unexcavated ancient site of Pirha and Lycian rural lifestyle.

ⓐ Bezirgan ⓣ 0242 837 5214 ⓦ www.owlsland.com ⓛ Tours daily in summer ❶ Admission charge; eight people max, with collection from Kalkan and lunch included

Kaputaş Gorge

Cuts from the coastline deep into the Lycian foothills. Several companies run canyoning routes down the river for a high-action morning or afternoon (see Kaş for details, page 47).

ⓐ 7 km (4 miles) east of Kalkan

Boat trips

Kalkan has a great range of boat trips, and you could probably spend two or three days exploring the different routes on offer. The trips also

⬢ Relax in the shade in Kalkan

get you to locations, including several cave systems, that you can't reach by car or dolmuş.

The two caves of Güvercinlik and Güvercin Güvercinlik lies at the mouth of one of the few freshwater streams that cut through the Lycian Mountains, making the water cooler than in other caves. It is also home to a population of wild pigeons and is an important bat roost. Güvercin cave is 40 m (44 yds) long and 30 m (100 ft) high, but is too narrow at the entrance for a tour boat to go inside. ⓐ 5 km (3 miles) along the coast

The Blue Cave This is the largest sea cave in Turkey, famed for the deep blue colour of the water (best seen from inside the cave looking out). The cave used to be a habitat for rare Mediterranean seals, but they have disappeared since the boat trips started.

Other tours Alternative boat tours often head out around the small **Rat and Snake Islets** just offshore. You could stop at **Pınar Kürü**, a pine-shaded rocky bay with very clear water that's ideal for snorkelling, or visit **Kaputaş beach** – the best in the area – where you can also explore **Kaputaş Gorge** just inland, or **Gerenlik Bay**, which has a reasonable sandy beach and is usually deserted because there's no access for vehicles.

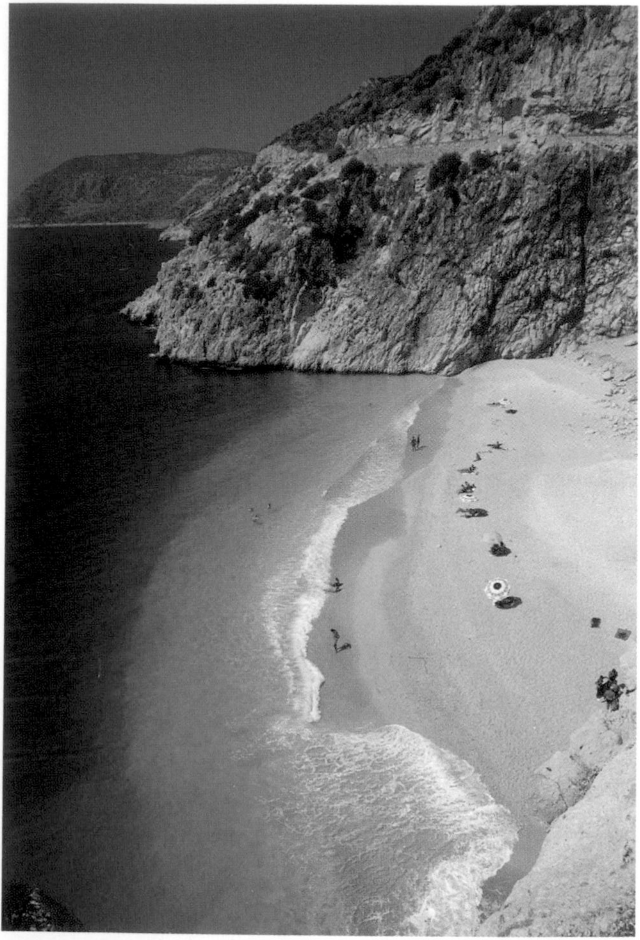

Take a dip in the crystal-clear waters

Other favoured anchorages are **Firnaz Bay**, a natural harbour 20 minutes out of Kalkan, or **French Bay** (east of Kalkan Bay), a popular stop for a swim.

Dolmuş services

There are local dolmuş services that go to **Saklıkent Gorge** (see page 63). They also frequently run to **Gelemiş/Patara** (see page 87), **Fethiye** (see page 21), **Kale/Demre** (see page 82) and **Kaş** (see page 45).

TAKING A BREAK

Merkez Café £ This is a great place to come and fill up on inexpensive Turkish snacks, such as *pide*, pizzas and kebabs. It's right in the heart of town, so is ideal for a lunch stop or to ward off the post-beach hunger pangs. ⓐ 2 Nolu Sokak ⓛ 08.00–24.00

Doy Doy ££ You will find excellent *meze* and Turkish salads in this restaurant, plus a good choice of fresh seafood, all with views over the port. ⓐ Yalıboyu Mah ⓣ 0242 844 3114 ⓛ 11.00–24.00

Kaptan Restaurant ££ Enjoy local dishes and fresh seafood at this small, family-owned restaurant. ⓐ Yalıboyu Mah ⓣ 0242 844 3166 ⓛ 11.00–24.00

Paprika Restaurant ££ Some of the best pasta dishes in the region are found at this courtyard restaurant, along with a range of local dishes. ⓐ 1 Nolu Sokak ⓣ 0242 844 1136 ⓛ 18.00–24.00 ❶ Booking is advised due to its popularity

Korsan £££ This is about the oldest restaurant in town, having drawn the crowds since the late 1970s. It is the perfect place to start your exploration of Turkish cuisine, with good-quality dishes served in a smarter setting than the usual *lokanta* without being overpriced for its beachside setting. ⓐ Yalıboyu Mah ⓣ 0242 844 3622 ⓛ 11.00–24.00

Ottoman House £££ Good Turkish cuisine is served in a lovely setting and the roof is decorated in the old Ottoman style. After your meal, you can enjoy a *nargile* (hubble-bubble pipe) with your Turkish coffee.
ⓐ Yalıboyu Mah 35 ⓣ 0242 844 1013 ⓛ 18.00–24.00

AFTER DARK

Kalkan isn't known for its loud nightlife. Most after-dinner entertainment involves enjoying a drink and conversation at a waterside café or bar.

Yacht Point This is the must-visit late-night music spot on the waterfront. Earlier in the evening, it's a great place to sit with a drink and people-watch. ⓐ Yalıboyu Mah ⓛ 11.00–03.00

⬥ *Enjoy a drink or light meal outdoors*

Kaş

Kaş (pronounced Kash) has the most dramatic setting of any Lycian resort, lying in the shadow of jagged Ak Dağlar mountain. Its name means 'eyebrow' or 'something curved' and is taken from the shape of its setting at the head of a curved natural inlet.

Clinging to its rocky coastline like a limpet, this tiny settlement of narrow cobbled streets and whitewashed Ottoman houses drips with pink bougainvillea and is surrounded by azure waters to the south and pristine pine-forested peaks to the north.

The first foreign tourists to discover Kaş were hippies and sailors, and the town still has the most relaxed and offbeat feel of any Turkish resort. This is for low-energy holidays – for high energy, head to **Hisarönü** or **Marmaris**. Kaş keeps its character because, even today, it is a sailor's paradise and the most difficult Lycian resort to reach by road. It has the longest transfer from both Antalya and Dalaman airports to the east and west, so it rarely gets swamped by vast numbers of tourists.

HISTORY

Kaş was ancient Antiphellos, an important Lycian trading town and port. Later it became a quiet backwater, a mostly rural community where families fished in the winter and, during the summer months, raised sheep and grew crops on the plateau behind the Lycian mountains.

In the late 18th century, Kaş and Kastellorizo (the tiny island just off shore) were an important centre for shipbuilding, mainly controlled by the Greek section of the population. During this time, many of the fine mansions of the town were built. After the exchange of Greek and Turkish populations in the 1920s, Kaş settled back into anonymity.

During the 1930s, Kaş was rediscovered by Turkish intellectuals, but there was not a decent road around the Lycian coast until well into the 20th century, so it remained a remote region – everything had to come in and go out by boat. In the 1960s, word got out about this fantastic hidden gem, and Kaş became one of the most popular locations on the 'hippy trail'.

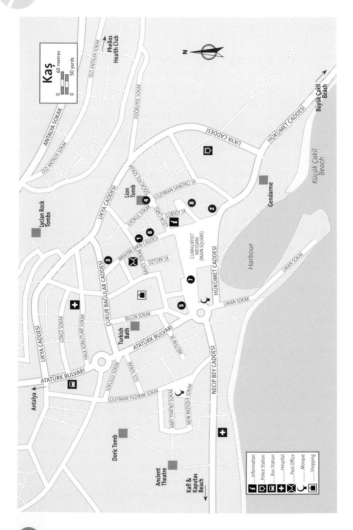

Kaş

0 — 60 metres
0 — 50 yards

OLD ANTALYA SOKAK
Phellos Health Club
ANTALYA SOKAK
OLD ANTALYA SOKAK

Büyük Çakıl Beach
HÜKÜMET CADDESİ
LİKYA CADDESİ
DOĞRUYOL SOKAK

Küçük Çakıl Beach

Lycian Rock Tombs
LİKYA CADDESİ
UZUN ÇARŞI SOKAK
Lion Tomb ❹
SÜLEYMAN SANDIKÇI SK.
❽
❷
Gendarme

LİKONU SOKAK
❻ ❶
YENİ CAMİ SK. GÜRSOY SK.
ℹ

Harbour

İBRAHİM SERİN CADDESİ
BAHÇE SK.
❾
ÖZTÜRK SK.

CUMHURİYET MEYDANI (MAIN SQUARE)

CUKUR BAĞILAR CADDESİ
❼
LİMAN SOKAK

LİKYA CADDESİ
BİLGİN SOKAK
❺
HÜKÜMET CADDESİ

GÖKLE SOKAK
HALK KONUTLARI SOKAK
Turkish Bath
ATATÜRK BULVARI
MECTAŞ SK.

LİMAN SOKAK

SOLULU SOKAK
ATATÜRK BULVARI
SÜLEYMAN YILDIRIM SOKAK
GÜL SOKAK

Antalya

NECİP BEY CADDESİ

AMFİ TİYATRO SOKAK
NEW MOSQUE SOKAK

Doric Tomb

Ancient Theatre
Kafi & Kaputas Beach

ℹ .... Information
🏛 .... Police Station
🚌 .... Bus Station
✚ .... Hospital
✉ .... Post Office
☾ .... Mosque
◼ .... Shopping

N

BEACHES

The beaches here are poor compared to resorts in the west of the Lycian region, and most swimming is from the coastal rocks or in artificial lidos.

THINGS TO SEE & DO

Trips
Boat trips are the best way to appreciate the wild beauty of the coast around Kaş, leading to many remote coves that are inaccessible by car, including the largest sea cave in Turkey, the **Blue Cave** (see page 41). There are also regular minibus trips to the long, turtle-nesting beach at **Patara**, where you can spend the day sunbathing or exploring the ancient remains just inland amongst the dunes (see page 87). Other popular destinations include the easily accessible, offshore islets of **Liman Ağzi** and **Kekova**.

For more information, contact **Kaş tourist office** ⓐ Cumhuriyet Meydanı 5 ⓣ 0242 836 123

Ancient theatre
The ancient theatre in Kaş is small by the standards of others in Turkey, but has been renovated.

Büyük Çakıl
A pebble beach that is not big, but it is busy because of its relatively easy walk from town.
ⓐ 1½ km (1 mile) east of town

Canyoning
Not for the faint-hearted, canyoning involves launching yourself down a river or stream, over chutes and waterfalls – no kayaks or rafts are involved! Trips from Kaş head into the Kaputaş Canyon 20 km (12 miles) west of town.

Doric Tomb

Cut into the hillside that forms the back of the theatre, this tomb was carved in the 3rd century BC.

Kaputaş Beach

This small beach is reached by car or small boat. Its dramatic setting at the mouth of a high gorge makes it a popular spot for sunbathers and yachts. There are few facilities here, so it is best to bring a picnic.
ⓐ 20 km (12 miles) west of town

Küçük Çakıl

The town beach is small, but is backed by hotels that can supply any refreshments you might need.

Lion Tomb

One of the largest Lycian tombs in the region, Lion Tomb sits squarely at an intersection in the middle of town and is usually draped with carpets for sale at the surrounding shops. It gets its name from the handles of the tomb lid, which are carved into the shape of lions' heads.

AGENCIES FOR ACTIVITIES

Bougainville Travel This English/Turkish company offers a full range of tours, but is respected for its activity-based excursions including canyoning, mountain biking, paragliding and trekking.
ⓐ Çukurbağlı Caddesi 10 ❶ 0242 836 3737
Ⓦ www.bougainville-turkey.com

Dolce Vita This rival company offers similar day tours, plus day trips to Kastellorizo (see opposite). ⓐ Cumhuriyet Meydanı 7
❶ 0242 836 1610 Ⓦ www.dolcevitatravel.org

Sea kayaking

You can travel to Üçağız for a day of kayaking in the azure waters of Kekova Sound (see page 76), with time to explore Kayaköy and the ancient remains of the Sunken City at closer quarters than on a tour boat. No experience needed.

Spa & Turkish baths

The **Phellos Health Club** has a modern *hamam* and spa for relaxation and massage.

ⓐ Doğru Yol Sokak ⓣ 0242 836 1953 ❶ Admission charge

Swimming with dolphins

The **Dolphin Therapy Centre** offers the opportunity to swim with these fabulous mammals (see Excursions, page 61).

Trekking

Kaş is right at the heart of the Lycian Way walking trail (see page 106). You can book guided walks for short sections close to the town to learn more about the history, flora and fauna of the region.

EXCURSIONS
Day trips to Kastellorizo

Lying tantalisingly close to the shoreline – it looks as if you could throw a stone to it, but is actually about three nautical miles – is the Greek island of **Kastellorizo**, also known in Greek as Megisti and in Turkish as Meis.

A remote outpost of the Dodecanese Islands (the same group as Rhodes and Kos), it was wealthy throughout the 19th century as a centre of shipbuilding and trade in high-quality sponges. There are some fine patrician mansions built by the leading families of the day on the waterfront of the main town, though many of these have a rather faded and careworn feel. There's a 14th-century castle of the Knights of St John and a small town museum. There was once an ancient site here, but the stones have been reused for the castle and the Church of Sts Constantine and Helena, erected in the 19th century.

> ## SHOPPING
>
> Although it is a small resort, Kaş has some of the most interesting and unusual shopping opportunities along the Turkish coast. This is partly a legacy of its old hippy days, but also because it is a high-class resort attracting wealthy Turks with money to spend. The old mansions in the main streets have been converted into boutiques selling locally designed high-quality clothing, jewellery, antiques and, of course, carpets. It is a very atmospheric place to shop, especially in the evenings.
>
> These individual boutiques have been joined by European high-street names – genuine here – such as Benetton and Naf Naf. There is also a bustling Friday market.

There are companies running day trips to the island from the harbour at Kaş (see box on page 48).

The Elmalı Plains
If you rent a car or hire a taxi for the day, it is worth heading inland. Once you climb up and over the **Ak Dağlar Mountains** that hem Kaş into the coastline, you reach a totally different landscape – a rich, fertile plain famed for its apple crops.

You'll need a four-wheel-drive vehicle to reach **Green Lake** high in the arid hills, as the steep road skirts the side of the hill and the surface is very loose. The lake, which was once a pilgrimage site, can totally dry up in summer, but the vistas are worth the trip. The small stone buildings on the plateau were seasonal shelters for shepherds who used to tend the herds here in summer.

Gömbe makes an interesting stop with its traditional local market, while **Sütleğen** sits at 1,500 m (5,000 ft), surrounded by mature pines and mountain scenery.

The town of **Elmalı** is low-key and not at all touristy. It has an interesting old quarter filled with cobbled lanes lined with Ottoman mansions plus a 17th-century mosque.

● *Spices at the market*

Dolmuş services

There are local dolmuş services to **Xanthos** (see page 84), **Letoön** (see page 79), **Fethiye** (see page 21), **Kalkan** (see page 37) and **Kale/Demre** (see page 82).

TAKING A BREAK

Cafe Corner £ ❶ Let some time pass with a coffee and cakes. Café Merhaba, across the way, is equally inviting. ⓐ İbrahim Serin Caddesi ❶ 0242 836 1409 ❶ 08.00–23.00

Noel Baba Pastanesi £ ❷ An old-fashioned Turkish pastry house that has now expanded its menu to include savoury snacks. This place has long been popular with locals and is one of the best places in Kaş to watch the world go by, whatever the time of day. ⓐ Cumhuriyet Meydanı 14 (the main square) ❶ 0242 836 1225 ⓛ 08.00–01.00

Oba Restaurant £ ❸ A little out of the mainstream, up the hill in town, Oba serves authentic and good-value *meze*, plus a range of vegetarian main dishes. They cook fresh every day and you'll need to visit the kitchen to decide what you want. ⓐ Çukur Bağlılar Caddesi ❶ 0242 836 1687 ⓛ 11.00–24.00

Bahçe £–££ ❹ Excellent *meze* here, with traditional décor and a garden. ⓐ Uzun Çarşi Caddesi (next to the Lion Tomb) ❶ 0242 836 2370 ⓛ 11.00–15.00 & 18.00–24.00

Chez Evy £££ ❺ The food here is French and delicious, including dishes such as crêpe suzette or coq au vin. ⓐ Terzi Sokak 2 ❶ 0242 836 1253 ⓛ 18.00–23.00 summer; 18.00–21.00 Tues–Sat winter

AFTER DARK

Harry's Bar ❻ One of Kaş's trendy bars, with a friendly but relaxed welcome, where everyone gathers for an early- or-late-evening drink. ⓐ İbrahim Serin Caddesi 13 ❶ 0242 836 1379 ⓛ 11.00–03.00

Mavi Bar ❼ This bar has remained a constant feature of the Kaş scene for the last few years. It is a relaxed café/bar with outdoor seating and a great view of the main square and waterfront. ⓐ Cumhuriyet Meydanı ⓛ 09.00–03.00

Secret Garden ❽ Drinks from 16.00 for a happy hour until 18.00 but the garden itself opens at 20.00. Water pipes and sofas define the scene. ⓐ İbrahim Serin Sokak 12 ❶ 0242 836 1533 ⓛ 16.00–02.00

Turunç

Set in a dramatic cove surrounded by craggy bluffs, Turunç (pronounced *Turunch*) is a picturesque resort, with its curved golden beach and hotels and *pansiyons* dotted around the pine-clad hills. There is still an air of exclusivity here as you drop into the resort, leaving the noise and bustle of Marmaris behind to find a slower, gentler pace of life.

Whilst Turunç is not for those who want to be in the centre of the action, you can still link up with any excursion that travels from the larger resort. It is perfect for those who want a medium-sized resort, but with the possibility of dipping into Turkey's most energetic beach- and nightlife.

Although the surrounding hills and coves hide the remains of many ancient settlements, the resort itself doesn't have a long history, developing as a small fishing village before eventually moving into tourism.

⏶ *The beach at Turunç is good for children*

BEACHES

The town beach is a beautiful curved sand and shingle strand – one of the best in the area – but for that reason it can be very busy with boat trippers from Marmaris. The shallow incline makes it good for children and non-swimmers, and the watersports opportunities are good.

For a little more peace and quiet, head to **Kumlubük** around the bay. Much of the land here is privately owned by one man, so you don't get many hotels and apartments and can escape the crowds.

THINGS TO SEE & DO

Boat trips

There are regular boat taxis to Turunç's bustling sister resort of **Marmaris**. Most people also spend at least one day enjoying a boat-taxi trip to the beaches of the peaceful neighbouring bays. The Five-Bays trip is the most popular from the harbour at Turunç, out into the **Bay of Marmaris**, including the famous **Cleopatra Island** (see page 16).

Outdoor activities

Erokoy Tours offer a range of sporting activities, from horse riding through the pine forests to sea kayaking in the calm bays.
ⓐ Kayabal Caddesi 40, İçmeler ⓣ 0252 455 5522
ⓦ www.anatoliandiscovery.com

Walks

The whole of the **Bozburun** peninsula is excellent for walking and hiking, and there are a number of marked paths leading from the resort. The bay of **Amos** is about an hour's walk along the coast road, with **Kumlubük** about 30 minutes further on. Alternatively, head into the hills; just remember to take some water and to wear suitable strong footwear.

EXCURSIONS
Ancient Amos

Amos is an ancient Rhodian and Hellenistic settlement and once had a population of 15,000 people. Today there remains little more than parts of the Acropolis, a temple, an untidy theatre and a few sections of wall. However, the beautiful views across the water with its sprinkling of islands and inlets make the trip worthwhile, and you'll probably have the place to yourself.

Around the Bozburun peninsula

The Bozburun peninsula south of the resort is the perfect place for exploration with a rental car. Here you will find tiny coastal villages in which to enjoy a relaxing seafood lunch, plus the remains of ancient places such as Ceresse, Paridon, Saranda, Tymuns and, at the very southern tip, Loryma.

TAKING A BREAK

Çınar Restaurant £ A great choice for good-value Turkish cuisine, Çınar is at the heart of the resort, so you can watch the world go by. ❸ Sokak 22 ❶ 0252 476 7123 ❷ 11.00–24.00

Minem ££ A neat restaurant and bar right on the beach; best late at night. ❸ Beach ❶ 0252 476 7285 ❷ 11.00–01.00

AFTER DARK

Habit Bar This family-run bar is where everybody meets early or late in the evening. Cihan, the owner, does great cocktails. Food is also available, so you could spend all evening here. ❷ H Mustafa Can Caddesi ❶ 0252 476 7581 ❷ 11.00–03.00

İçmeler

İçmeler (pronounced ich-miller) sits in one of the most picturesque bays on the Bozburun peninsula to the west of Marmaris. It boasts a sheltered golden beach shaded by palm trees, backed by forested hills and looking out on numerous offshore islands. It has developed fast since the early 1990s, but still has touches of the old ways of life, with traditional houses set amongst the modern hotels.

BEACHES

The resort beach of golden sand and small shingle runs around the bay, and there are several café bars right on the beach so you don't need to move far for lunch or drinks. There is also an ample selection of watersports – both motorised and non-motorised – to enjoy.

THINGS TO SEE & DO

Little Train
Really this is just another form of public transport to get holidaymakers around the resort, but it is a good way to get your bearings and one of the cheapest tours you can get.

SHOPPING
The canal that runs through İçmeler has shops along its length and is a particularly romantic place to shop in the evenings, when a ribbon of lights adds a golden glow. There is also a good market on Wednesdays, but İçmeler is so close to Marmaris and its amazing shopping opportunities that most people head there to spend their holiday cash!

● *Içmeler beach*

Boat rides

Take the water taxi to **Marmaris** (see pages 15–20). This is a great form of public transport that is worth taking just for the ride. It runs several times every day in peak season.

From the waterfront in town you have the same choice of trips as those available from Marmaris. Head to **Turunç** (see page 53) for a more low-key resort atmosphere, or to the southwest beyond Turunç for empty bays for great swimming and snorkelling.

Diving

Diver's Delight This company, which has been open since the late 1980s, runs 'Try-a-Dive' days and PADI qualification courses.

ⓐ Kayabal Caddesi 63 ❶ 0252 455 3885 ⓦ www.diversdelight.com

Spa & Turkish baths

Hotel Aqua This spa offers various massages, body wraps and aromatherapy treatments, plus ayurveda and yoga sessions for total relaxation.

ⓐ Sahil Sokak 5 ☏ 0252 455 3636 Ⓦ www.hotelaqua.com

EXCURSIONS

You can easily get involved in any of the excursions from **Marmaris** (see page 19) and **Turunç** (see page 55).

TAKING A BREAK

Küçük Ev £ Very well-established restaurant serving good-value set meals. ⓐ Altın Sahil ☏ 0252 455 1200 ⏲ 11.00–23.00

Golden Beach Restaurant ££ Directly on the beach and open throughout the day, Golden Beach offers a great venue for lunch, dinner or drinks, with views across the water. Live music every night from 20.00.
ⓐ Altın Sahil ☏ 0252 455 4670 ⏲ 08.00–01.00

Majestic Restaurant ££ Voted best restaurant in town a number of times, the Majestic has a mixed menu including both European and Asian dishes. ⓐ Cumhuriyet Mah, Osman Gazi Caddesi 30 ☏ 0252 455 2740 ⏲ 11.00–02.00

AFTER DARK

Starlight Nights Unusual to see in Turkey, Starlight Nights offers Las Vegas-style revue shows (three shows to suit different age groups) with glamorous sequin-clad dancers. Dinner and your first drink are included in the price. Tickets are available through your holiday representative or tour agent in the resort. ⏲ From 19.00 during the season

◑ *White-water rafting on the Dalaman River is great fun!*

EXCURSIONS
Out & about

Lycian adventures

THINGS TO SEE & DO

Jeep or 4x4 safari

The jeep safari is a real adventure. Out and about on roads you'd never venture to in a rental car, it gives you a chance to see the traditional Turkish way of life and discover the countryside surrounding your resort. Routes vary with each company, but the following gives you an idea of where you might like to go.

In the mountains behind **Kaş**, you can tour the lands around the farming villages of **Uğrar**, **Sütleğen** and **Gökçeören**, with a stop for lunch in a village house.

Fethiye has some excellent inland locations that are also easily reached from **Hisarönü** and **Ölüdeniz**. Ancient **Tlos** or the hills around **Baba Dağı** offer exciting overland journeys.

From Marmaris, İçmeler and Turunç, the **Hisarönü** and **Datça peninsulas** are open to you. There are breathtaking unspoilt coves and forested hillsides (some areas are still recovering from devastating fires in the 1990s) to explore. Very sparsely populated, the countryside provides a lovely contrast to the busy resorts.

Microlighting

If you'd rather take an aerial tour of the **Ölüdeniz** area under the power of an engine than simply under a parachute, try microlighting. These small, manoeuvrable craft offer you a bird's-eye view over the mountains and offshore, but you sit in a seat at the side of a qualified pilot rather than dangling from a harness. **Fly South** offer flights from the runway at Hisarönü.

❶ Book with your holiday representative or a local agency.

Paragliding

One of the most awe-inspiring and exhilarating ways to experience the Turkish coast is by being strapped to a qualified paraglider and jumping off a Lycian mountain. Don't worry, you will be given some instruction about what to do before you take the leap of faith, then you will be guided down in a journey that lasts over an hour. Two areas to try are:

Mount Baba If you are staying in Ölüdeniz, Hisarönü or Fethiye, try the trip from the summit of Mount Baba above Ölüdeniz. This is the longest paragliding drop in the world, at 1,900 m (3,250 ft). You will spiral down over the teardrop beach and its limpid lagoon, but not before you've enjoyed the staggering long-distance views. Contact **Sky Sports** in Ölüdeniz. ☎ 0252 617 0511 Ⓦ www.skysports-turkey.com

Mount Asaz There is a launch area close to the summit of Mount Asaz, near Kaş, with a 1,000-m (3,300-ft) drop. The descent offers incredible views over the Lycian coastline and across to the island of Kaştellorizo just offshore, before landing back in the centre of Kaş just by the harbour. **Bougainville Travel** (see page 48) organises jumps.

ⓘ Your normal travel insurance does not cover you for tandem paragliding, so make sure you choose a reputable company with good insurance.

Swimming with dolphins

The **Dolphin Therapy Centre** has been running carefully supervised programmes for children with mental and physical disabilities in conjunction with a medical institute in Russia. This work is still carrying on, but now the centre is also running swim-with-the-dolphins sessions for the public. You can spend 15–20 minutes in the water with a bottlenose dolphin or simply watch the activities from the viewing gantry if you do not want to swim. The centre is situated in Kaş, but the ticket agent is in Fethiye and runs transport from there to Kaş. This means that the excursion is easy to join from other resorts, such as Ölüdeniz, Hisarönü and Fethiye, as well as Kaş and Kalkan.
Contact **Gala Yachting & Travel** ⓐ Cumhuriyet Mah, Sokak 503, Fethiye
☎ 0252 614 6716 Ⓦ www.delphintherapie.net

White-water rafting on the Dalaman River

This is just about the most energetic and exhilarating activity you can find along the Turkish coast. Dalaman River rafting is world famous for

its challenging grade-four rapids. However, many sections are not very difficult, so if you are a rafting virgin it is the perfect place to start. There is enough white water here to get your adrenalin rushing, but plenty of quiet spells in between for you to catch your breath and take in the wonderful views.

The journey to the rafting departure point (1.5 hours from Fethiye or Marmaris) is also spectacular, with a route through the **Taurus Mountains** offering dramatic landscapes and a glimpse of rural lifestyles.

The large rafts can carry about 15 people, so they are perfect for a group. You will get a guide to show you the basics and will be kitted out with all the necessary safety gear. Then there will be a bit of singing to get you in the party mood before it's 'paddles at the ready'. All the rafts stay together on the river and the guides are on hand to make sure the trip is safe and fun.

The rafting starts quietly before leading through several sections of rapids with names like Rockgate, Long Rapid, Slingshot and Nazaretme, where you'll need to use all your new-found skills.

All this excitement really builds an appetite, so you will appreciate the simple lunch of barbecued meats and delicious fresh trout plus salads and fruit to build up your energy levels again.

After swimming in the rock pools or a spot of sunbathing, you will carry on down the river, under the ancient Roman bridge, before reaching the village of **Akköprü**, the end of the trip.

The travel company **Alternatif Turizm** (see page 18) in Marmaris runs well-organised rafting tours, with pick-ups from along the Lycian coast. They also offer river and sea kayaking, canyoning, hiking and mountain biking.

❶ Children under six years old are not allowed to ride in the rafts for safety reasons.

Saklıkent Gorge

A dramatic landscape feature, Saklıkent Gorge cuts 18 km (11 miles) into the Akdağlar Mountains, carved by the power of water and wind.

THINGS TO SEE & DO

Saklıkent Gorge floor

You can walk for 2 km (1¼ miles) along the gorge floor. Any further exploration requires ropes and climbing equipment! There is a metal walkway along the first 150 m (165 yds) where the gorge is at its widest, and you'll reach a shady restaurant by the water's edge. From here you have to paddle through the freezing water to reach the gorge floor. The sheer walls are curved into all sorts of surreal shapes. In certain places you'll have to climb through narrow boulder-strewn gaps and rock pools.

At the mouth of the gorge there are several restaurants by the river with wooden verandas overhanging the water. This is a wonderfully atmospheric place to enjoy a drink or a lunch of fresh trout.

🚍 40 km (25 miles) east of Fethiye 🕓 Sunrise–sunset
ℹ Admission charge

TURKISH EVENING

Genuine Turkish food and entertainment may be difficult to find in many modern resorts, but the 'Turkish evening' offers the perfect introduction to the culture and it's a really fun evening out. You'll start with a buffet meal of *meze* dishes, barbecued meats and salads, washed down with local wine or beer (see page 96 for more details of traditional foods). After dinner you will be entertained by a troupe performing local folkloric dances plus of course the famous belly dance, regarded by the Ottomans as the height of eroticism. Someone from the audience is always invited to have a go, which is usually hilarious. Later in the evening, the dance floor is handed over to the guests for an hour or so of disco dancing.

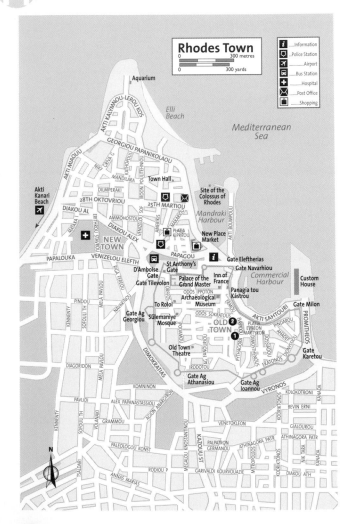

Rhodes Town

0 .... 300 metres
0 .... 300 yards

i .... Information
⊘ .... Police Station
✈ .... Airport
🚌 .... Bus Station
✚ .... Hospital
✉ .... Post Office
🛍 .... Shopping

Aquarium

Elli Beach

Mediterranean Sea

AKTI KALYMANOU-LEROU KOS

GEORGIOU PAPANIKOLAOU

ORFEA G

NIKI

MANDILARA

KATHOPOLI

IROON POLITECHNIOU

Akti Kanari Beach ✈

AKTI MIAOULI

DILMPERAKI

28TH OKTOVRIOU

SOF

VENIZELOU

AMERIKIS

DIAKOU ALEX

DIAKOU AL

MATAXA

NAVARINOU SOTIROU

AMMOHOSTOU

25TH MARTIOU

Town Hall

Site of the Colossus of Rhodes

Mandraki Harbour

AKTI BOUMOLI

✚

⊘

✉

PLATIA KIPROU

New Place Market

NEW TOWN

⊘

PAPAGOU

i

Gate Eleftherias

PAPALOUKA

VENIZELOU ELEFTH

🚌

St Anthony's Gate

D'Amboise Gate

Gate Tilevolon

Palace of the Grand Master

Inn of France

Gate Navarhiou

Commercial Harbour

Custom House

PINDOU

MELA PAVLOU

AGIA TEREGU

NAVARINOU

ORFEOS

ODOS IPPOTON

Archaeological Museum

Panagia tou Kástrou

ERMU

Gate Milon

KENNEDY

SOFOULI TH

Gate Ag Georgiou

Süleymaniye Mosque

To Roloi

ODOS SOKRATOUS

OLD TOWN

PLATIA EVREON MARTYRON

AKTI SAHTOURI

PINDAROU

AGISSANDROU

PROMITHEOS

DIMOKRATIAS

Old Town Theatre

PYTHAGORA

PYTHAGORA

HANDARIOU

IRODOTOU

Gate Karetou

DIAGORIDON

MELA PAVLOU

KOMNINON

Gate Ag Athanasiou

Gate Ag Ioannou

VYRONOS

EKATONOS

DIONISIOU

KOLOKOTRONI

KANADA

PAVLIDI

ALEX PAPANASTASSIOU

AGION ANASTON

BEVIN ERNI

KENNEDY

GRAMMOU

VOJANAKI

MEGALOU KONSTANTINOU

25 KOZYRI

VENETOKLEON

PALPATRON GERMANOU

ATHINAGORA PATR

KOSKINONOS

GIALOUROU

KODRIKTONOS

NIK TAPA

KANADA

PALEOLOGOU KONST

RODIOU P

ANNAS MARIAS

N

TSALDARI

GARIVALDI KOURVOUAZIE

MITROPOLEOS

DIAKOU ATH

Rhodes Town

The Greek island of Rhodes is one of the jewels of the eastern Mediterranean. Its unique old town makes an interesting day trip, most easily taken from Marmaris, or from much of the western region.

HISTORY

The immense citadel of Rhodes Town was the headquarters of the Knights of St John from 1309. The knights provided medical care for pilgrims on journeys to the Holy Land, but later became one of the leading medieval military organisations and the front line against the forces of Islam coming from the East. In 1522, after a long siege, Ottoman forces took Rhodes and held it until 1912. Following the Italian–Turkish War, the island was ceded to Italy. It then became part of Greece in 1947.

THINGS TO SEE & DO

The town walls

The high sandstone walls are 4 km (2½ miles) long. Seven of the original eight gates still remain in use today, the most interesting being the **d'Amboise Gate** in the northwest corner, built in 1512. This curves in an 'S' shape to outwit attackers and is linked to a second gate, **St Anthony's**, which lies between two inner curtain walls. The **Sea Gate**, closest to the port, is the most impressive, flanked by two massive round towers. A walk around the walls takes approximately 40 minutes.

The Knights' Quarter or Collachium

The old town is divided into two sectors: the Collachium, where the knights lived, and the Chora, where the rest of the population lived. The Collachium dates back to 1309 and is a good place to begin.

Panagía tou Kástrou (The Church of Our Lady of the Castle)

This 14th-century building used to be the knights' cathedral. It was converted into a mosque during the Ottoman period, and local Rhodians

call it the Red Church because of massacres that took place inside when the Muslims arrived. Today it is home to the **Museum of Religious Art in the Post-Byzantine Period**, displaying a collection of icons from the 14th, 15th and 20th centuries.

ⓐ Platía Moussíou (Museum Square) ⓛ 08.30–15.00 Tues–Sun
❶ Admission charge

Archaeological Museum of Rhodes

The museum is housed in the 15th-century Knights' Hospital. The medieval building was state-of-the-art for its time. Inside, **The Infirmary Room** houses relics of the era of the knights, with gravestones and coats of arms of illustrious members on display.

The rest of the rooms display ancient statuary and other artefacts from various Dodecanese islands, many of which were excavated during the Italian Period. The grave *stele* of Krito and Tamerista, carved around 410 BC by a local artist, is one of the most renowned exhibits.

ⓐ Platía Moussíou ⓛ 08.00–19.00 Tues–Sun Apr–Oct; 08.30–15.00 Tues–Sun Nov–Mar ❶ Admission charge

Odós Ippotón (Street of the Knights)

This is one of the most complete medieval streets in the world, with a long façade of fine, carved stonemasonry on which many small details can be seen. The **Inn of France** is the most highly decorated and its internal courtyard has a chapel dating from *c.* 1374, though the street frontage dates from over 100 years later.

Palace of the Grand Master

This was the administrative heart and power base of the Order of the Knights of St John. Dating from the late 15th century, it was badly damaged by an explosion in 1856 and was renovated by the Italians.

The ground-floor rooms, which originally acted as stables and grain and munitions stores, are reached across a courtyard sporting a series of classical statues. They house a permanent exhibition of finds from 2,400 years of Rhodes' history, plus other temporary exhibitions. Many of the

◆ *Palace of the Grand Master*

major rooms on the upper floors have beautiful Hellenistic, Roman and early-Christian mosaics taken from the neighbouring island of Kos. These include one depicting the nine muses and another showing the head of the Medusa. Though it is ethically questionable whether they should be here, they have been carefully preserved and look spectacular.

ⓐ Top of Odós Ippotón ⏰ 12.30–20.00 Mon, 08.00–20.00 Tues–Sun July–Oct; 08.30–15.00 Tues–Sun Nov–June ❶ Admission charge

The Chora or Town

The Knights lived in the Collachium, but a thriving town developed within the city walls and much of this remains as it was during the Ottoman era. This quarter is a maze of stone alleyways, some bustling, others deserted. Stone archways spanning the lanes add a particular character and also serve the serious function of providing structural support during earthquakes. Take your time to explore here – streets such as Fanouriou, Pithagora and Sophocleous make good starting points.

Süleymaniye Mosque

Built in 1523 to mark the Ottoman takeover of the island, the mosque has been renovated. Climb the small flight of steps at the back for the best views of the large dome that tops the building.

ⓐ Odós Panetiou ❶ Not open to the public

To Roloi

Climb to the top of this clock tower, erected in 1851, for impressive views over the rooftops of the Old Town. From here you can clearly see what a maze it is.

ⓐ Odós Panetiou ⏰ 08.00–22.00 ❶ Admission charge

Odós Sokratous (Socrates Street)

The main shopping thoroughfare in Ottoman times, Odós Sokratous, is at first glance, just as it was 150 years ago, thronging with people bargaining for goods in many languages and shopkeepers willing to do a little bartering to secure a sale. Of course, times have changed –

the constant ring of mobile phones reminds you that you're in the 21st century.

Platía Ippokrátous (Hippocrates Square)

One of the main meeting places in the Old Town, Platía Ippokrátous is decorated by a Sintrivani fountain, topped by a miniature minaret. In the southeastern corner of the square, the stone building called the **Castellenia** (completed in 1507) was the medieval courthouse and stock exchange. It now houses the public library and town archives.

Platía Evréon Martyron (Square of the Jewish Martyrs)

This square is named in remembrance of the 2,000 Jewish people who lived in Rhodes Town when the Germans arrived in 1943 after Italian capitulation, of whom only 50 returned after the war. On the north side of the square are the old Naval Headquarters for the knights, which became the seat of the Christian Orthodox Church in Rhodes, now known as the **Archbishop's Palace**. The 16th-century **Kal de Shalom Synagogue** has been carefully renovated.

ⓐ Odós Dosaidou, just off the square

TAKING A BREAK

Taverna Kostas £–£££ ❶ Off the beaten tourist track on an old, narrow street, Taverna Kostas has been run by the same family for over 30 years. It is popular with locals for its authentic cuisine. Relax in the lovely terrace garden over a meal or a snack. ⓐ Odós Pythagora 62 ⓣ 0241 26217 ⓛ 11.00–15.00 & 18.00–late ❗ Cash only

Fotis £££ ❷ This friendly seafood taverna in the heart of the old town ticks all the right boxes but it's well worth a visit for the top quality food and convivial atmosphere. A firm favourite of the locals but it can become pricey as you pay for your fish by the kilo. Indoor and outdoor seating areas are available. ⓐ 8 Menekleous, Old Town ⓣ 241 027 359 ⓛ 08.00-01.00

Antalya

The anchor city of the Mediterranean coast, Antalya is, aside from İstanbul, the most 'happening' city in the country, and it is the perfect place to capture the 'East meets West' clash of cultures that encapsulates modern Turkey.

HISTORY

The Persians founded Antalya in 158 BC on the site of a deep natural harbour. It was important throughout ancient times and came to be prized by the Romans and Byzantines because it was safe and gave them easy access to the whole eastern Mediterranean.

When the Ottomans took over the city in the 16th century, it was surrounded by a 5-km (3-mile) long wall. They divided the city into four districts, housing the Greek, Jewish and Muslim communities, and also the ruling classes or Mamelukes.

After the fall of the Ottoman Empire, the city was abandoned and its mansions became dilapidated, but since the 1980s it has undergone a huge programme of renovation and has been reborn as the largest medieval citadel along the Turkish tourist coast.

THINGS TO SEE & DO

Antalya Archaeological Museum

This is one of the best museums of ancient finds in the eastern Mediterranean. Even if you don't normally enjoy tramping around ancient ruins, you will be impressed by the amazing artefacts on display here. These have been brought from sites all around the Turkish Mediterranean.

The highlight of the museum is the collection of artefacts from the **ancient city of Perge** to the east of Antalya. This highly decorated, monumental statuary (mostly 2nd century AD) shows just how sophisticated the city must have been in its heyday. Look particularly for a beautiful statue of a dancer carved using two different marbles – her

◉ *Ancient statuary at Antalya Archaeological Museum*

light skin contrasting with her dark hair and dress. The collection of ornamental friezes that decorated the theatre at Perge is considered the finest of its type in the world.

The star of the museum's **Byzantine and Christian collection** is the reliquary that is said to have held the bones of the 4th-century AD Bishop of Myra, St Nicholas (or Noel Baba as he is known in Turkish), the saint on whom the modern legend of Santa Claus is based (see page 83). The collection also includes icons recovered from various churches after the Greek community left in the 1920s.

The museum also houses **Bronze Age finds** which include items from the 6th–8th centuries BC, when the Phrygian people inhabited the area. The best include statuary and funerary urns.

The most interesting area in this **ethnological collection** of Selçuk and Ottoman handicrafts is the diorama of a traditional nomadic lifestyle, showing how many Turks lived until the 20th century, and some still do.

ⓐ Cumhuriyet Caddesi ⏰ 09.00–18.00 Tues–Sun, closed Mon
❶ Admission charge

Antalya Beach Park

A fantastic concept for a city resort, Antalya Beach Park to the west of the downtown core is a huge pre-planned leisure area with a range of activities and some lovely natural areas to explore. There is a paintball arena, golf, parks and children's play areas, a range of food from snack kiosks to restaurants, plus access to Konyaaltı Beach for watersports. The two major attractions are: **Aqualand**, a huge waterpark with impressive rides with names like Twister and Black Hole, a massive wave pool and a children's play area; and **Dolphinland**, where you can watch the dolphin shows and even have the opportunity to swim with the dolphins.

ⓐ Dumlupınar Bul. Konyaaltı Koruluğu Yanı ❶ 0242 249 0900
ⓦ www.beachpark.com.tr

Kaleiçi (Old Quarter)

This medieval labyrinth of narrow alleyways and courtyarded mansions is still evocative of Ottoman Turkey, though its history dates back to before Roman times. Today the quarter is home to stylish boutique hotels, upmarket restaurants and bohemian shops.

There is no set route for sightseeing; just follow your nose around the next picture-perfect corner, browsing as you go. You will be able to explore excellent renovations and evocative ruins, but whether the mansion is a palace or the pits, the beauty is in the detail – wooden lintels, stone archways and a palate of weather-worn pastel stucco walls add to the atmosphere. Look out for the following highlights on your wanders around the old town:

City walls Various sections of the Roman city wall survive. At Kalekapısı, the main entrance to Kaleiçi, a section of wall supports Saat Kulesi, a Selçuk clock tower. Other sections run from the harbour around the rocky coastline, but the longest and most impressive stretch runs south of Hadrian's Gate (see below).

Hadrian's Gate Built at the eastern flank of Roman Antalya in AD 130, this triumphal arch celebrated a visit to the city by Emperor Hadrian. A flight of steps leading down to the gate shows just how much higher the modern city is than it was in Roman times.

The old harbour Down on the shore below the mansions of Kaleiçi, the harbour is now a pleasure marina with a flotilla of little boats offering tours of the bay. There are several cafés and restaurants, so it is a popular place for lunch. While you are relaxing, you can examine the walls of the harbour, which were built by the Romans and have been reinforced regularly since then.

Yivli Minare (Fluted Minaret) Built in 1230 by Sultan Alâeddin Keykubad, the fluted mosque, so-called because the minaret has a fluted tower, has become a symbol of Antalya. The mosque next door is still used for worship.

TAKING A BREAK

Anfi ££ Based in the harbour area, this is a very popular restaurant with the locals because it serves excellent food at reasonable prices. Try the *meze* dishes. It also has a large terrace. 🅐 Kaleiçi Yat Limanı (in the old port) 🕿 0242 243 2073 🕔 11.00–24.00

Antalya Balık Evi ££ Situated on the edge of Antalya's bustling market, this popular and friendly restaurant cooks whatever the fishing boats happen to bring in that day. 🅐 Eski Lara Yolu Lara 🕿 242 3231 823 🕔 All day

Dalyan boat trip

The Dalyan boat trip is one of most fun-filled excursions you can take and it brings everything that's great about a holiday in Turkey – a little bit of history, fantastic views, lots of wildlife, swimming and mud baths – together in one action-packed day.

Dalyan Çayı (Dalyan River) drains freshwater Köyceğiz Gölü (Lake Köyceğiz) and runs into the Mediterranean. The slow-moving river meanders between two high limestone bluffs, and its banks are lined with thick reed beds that support a wealth of bird life, such as storks and herons, plus fish and amphibians. As in ancient times, there are several fish farms along the banks, and delicious freshly grilled trout is a delicacy of the region.

🕐 Daily tours at 10.30 from Dalyan river docks, returning at 16.00

❶ Admission charge (plus separate charge for Kaunos site and mud baths)

BOAT TRIP SIGHTS

Lycian tombs

Across the river from Dalyan village is an impressive collection of Lycian tombs. They are numerous and incredibly elegantly carved, but most awe-inspiring is the fact that they sit high up on the cliff side with no obvious means of access, prompting the question – how did the ancient Lycians carve out the tombs without the aid of modern scaffolding?

Kaunos

These magnificent cliff tombs were the work of the people of ancient Kaunos. During ancient times, the city sat above a malaria-infested swamp (mosquitoes can still be a problem here but the malaria has been eradicated) and was said to be one of the most unhealthy places in the Roman Empire. The city made money from the ancient slave trade until the river silted up and the docks could no longer operate.

Most of the city hasn't been excavated. There are regular digs during the summer but progress is slow. The site offers excellent views out over the valley and along the river to the sea, which is now 5 km (3 miles) away. This is probably the highlight of the tour – especially if ancient remains aren't your thing.

The lower town has a Roman baths complex plus temples and an agora. The Acropolis has evidence of fortifications from the 3rd century BC to medieval times, plus a well-preserved Hellenistic theatre.

It is a 10-minute walk from the boat dock to the remains, and the route is steep in parts, so wear comfortable shoes and take some water with you.

İztuzu Beach

Your river trip continues seaward, where the next stop is *İztuzu Beach*, a spectacular 7-km (4½-mile) swathe of sand backed by scrub-covered dunes, whose western advance is narrowing the river's mouth. İztuzu is a major turtle-nesting beach and you may spot one of these shy creatures in the shallows during the egg-laying season between May and July.

Since these creatures are now endangered, please follow the guidelines to protect the nests. These are printed on panels around the site. The most important of these is not to enter the taped-off area where the eggs are located.

The sea here can have quite high waves because the bay is open to the prevailing winds, but the marshes behind the dunes have warm, calm pools, much more suited for swimming. These are also home to lots of wildlife species, including fantastic iridescent dragonflies, terrapins and the now rare Anatolian tortoise.

Ilıca mud baths

Said to be beneficial for rheumatism and male potency, most holiday-makers visit for the fun of smearing themselves in the warm brown goo!

Lake Köyceğiz

On the return journey to Dalyan, boats rest at Lake Köyceğiz and you can swim in the cool, fresh water.

Kekova boat trip

The coastal shallows of Kekova Sound in southeast Lycia make one of the most beautiful and popular day trips along this part of the coast. Kekova Island shelters crystal-clear waters and numerous rocky islets. The vista is topped off by the jagged, arid Lycian peaks just inland.

Until recently, this idyllic corner of the Turkish coast was the exclusive preserve of 'yachties' who could lay anchor in one of the many remote coves seemingly kilometres away from the rest of the world. Today, the pleasures of the area can be enjoyed by everyone for a lot less than the cost of a yacht charter – and with lunch included in the package.
🕐 Boat trips daily (weather permitting in winter) ❶ Admission charge (plus a charge for entering the castle)

Boat trips set off from all parts of the coast, east and west. The further you travel in the boat, the less time you'll have at Kekova, so you may not experience all the activities listed below. The itinerary here assumes that you have sailed from the closest port, Üçağız.

BOAT TRIP SIGHTS

Kekova Island
Kekova Island lies just a few hundred metres off shore and only became an island when the level of the Mediterranean rose in the early part of the first millennium. As the water flooded in, it swallowed the ancient city that thrived here. The city remains are called Batıkkent (the 'sunken city'), but archaeologists haven't yet identified which city it actually was.

The island is protected as an ancient site so no one is allowed to set foot on it, but your boat will get in close to shore and you can get good views of the remains of numerous stone buildings clinging to the hillside, and the ancient harbour just below the water line. Under the water are the remains of yet more buildings, and the sea bed is dotted with ancient pottery amphorae lying where they fell many hundreds of years ago.

The necropolis of Teimiussa

On the inland shoreline are the remains of ancient Teimiussa, half-submerged in water and half-choked by the fertile mud that now helps make this part of Turkey the capital of fruit and vegetable production. Look out particularly for several excellent Lycian tombs rising out of the water, supported on their stone pillars.

Kaleköy

Kaleköy (the ancient site of Simena) is one of the prettiest and most authentic villages along the Turkish coast, and the view as you approach from the water makes a perfect picture with a rash of traditional whitewashed houses climbing up the hillside, crowned by a sturdy fortress (see below).

Once your boat has moored at one of the numerous rustic wooden jetties, you are free to explore the narrow winding alleyways. The settlement is a fascinating mixture of living community and tourist town. Most of the houses are family homes and chickens roam free throughout the village, scattering noisily as you approach. The older women sit in their doorways crocheting or making the lace that is on sale everywhere; children offer fruit or small trinkets, while carpet shops simply hang their wares off balconies or over walls.

The Fortress of the Knights of St John

The fortress was built by the Knights of St John and offers wonderful high-level views over Kekova sound and the town. It's one of their smaller outposts but still a beautiful example of crusader architecture. 🕐 24 hours ❗ Admission charge when guardian is on duty

Swimming

After your explorations, you will be allowed time for swimming and snorkelling. Watch out for the spiny sea urchins that breed in the shallows here. If you step on them, the spines break off in your foot and can become infected.

▲ *Kekova harbour*

Letoön

Lycia's most important religious site, Letoön, was home to the shrine of the Lycians' major goddess Leto. It was also the site of a famed Oracle and played host to festivals organised by the cities that made up the Lycian Federation (one of the world's earliest democratic governments).

When Alexander the Great arrived in Letoön in 334 BC, the Oracle informed him that his forces would crush the Persians, which is just what they went on to do (and far more). Under the Romans, the shrine remained an important place of pilgrimage. Later, under the Byzantines, it was converted into a Christian basilica and thrived until Arab raiders pillaged the area in the 7th century. Charles Fellows discovered the site during his explorations of the 1840s but thankfully moved on to Xanthos (see page 84) to strip that city of its finest treasures. Letoön was only seriously excavated in the 1960s.

The site consists mainly of the remains of various temples. At the centre is a trio dedicated to Leto, Artemis and Apollo – the three major deities of the Lycians. The temple of Apollo has a fine mosaic floor featuring a lyre and a bow and arrow (symbolising Artemis and Apollo). 🕐 08.00–19.30 summer; 08.00–17.00 winter ❶ Admission charge

LETO'S STORY

Leto was a water nymph who caught the eye of Zeus (head of the Greek gods) and they embarked on a passionate affair. Leto became pregnant but was discovered by Zeus' wife, Hera, who banished her. As she wandered the countryside to find somewhere to give birth to the twins Apollo and Artemis, she found a spring on the site of Letoön, but was shunned by local herdsmen. Eventually she was led to drink at the River Xanthos by a family of wolves. The Greek word *lykos* – the derivation of Lycia – means wolf.

Tlos

Normally linked with Saklıkent Gorge (see page 63) on a day trip from the coast, Tlos was one of the Lycian Federation's most important cities.

The site has a magnificent setting, but it hasn't been excavated and archaeologists still aren't sure what all the buildings are.

ⓐ 22 km (14 miles) from Fethiye ⓛ 24 hours ❶ Admission charge if ticket collector present

THINGS TO SEE & DO

The baths complex

With its section of five-arched windows, this is one of the most complete sections of stonework at the site.

The theatre

With its backdrop of Lycian peaks, this is very atmospheric and has some finely carved seating still intact.

THE STORY OF BELLEROPHON

Bellerophon was wrongly accused by King Proteus of making advances towards his Queen. He was ordered to visit the land of neighbouring Iobates, King of Lycia, with a note saying 'kill this subject of mine'.

Iobates could not kill the boy outright but sent him on a series of supposedly impossible missions. However, when Bellerophon completed all the tasks asked of him, Iobates decided to tell him of the message and to take Bellerophon as an ally. When Iobates died, Bellerophon became King of Lycia.

◓ *The ancient theatre of Tlos*

Tomb of Bellerophon

Set amongst a series of Lycian rock-cut tombs is the so-called Bellerophon Tomb, a large and impressive example with a temple-style façade and a bas-relief depicting Bellerophon riding Pegasus, the winged horse. One of the ruling families of the city claimed descent from the mythical hero Bellerophon, and archaeologists assume this is their royal tomb.

Ottoman fortifications

To the right of the site as you approach, look for some fortifications that were built in the Ottoman era by a feudal-style ruler Ali Ağa, nicknamed 'Bloody' by the local population who suffered under his patronage.

Myra & Kale

The site at ancient Myra allows you to get up close to some of the best Lycian tombs in Turkey. The modern town of Kale (also known locally as Demre) close to the site has been a centre of pilgrimage for many centuries because it is the birthplace of St Nicholas – our Santa Claus or, as he is known in Turkey, Baba Noel.

HIGHLIGHTS

Dating back to the 5th century BC, Myra was one of the most important cities of the ancient Lycian people. It supplied a form of incense to the expanding Greek and Roman world. The city was finally abandoned after earthquake damage and much of the site is still to be excavated. Today there are three main areas to explore.

The Sea Necropolis
The main collection of tombs, known as the Sea Necropolis, are carved at eye level into the sheer cliff face. The tombs were carved to imitate the house of the subject during life, with an ornate door marking the entrance. Unlike at Dalyan (see page 74), you can get up close to the carvings to study the detail, but you can't go inside.

The theatre
Next to the tombs is a well-preserved theatre, one of the smallest at a major site in Turkey. The entrance galleries and stairs used by Roman audiences are still pretty much intact, so you can climb them and imagine you are going to take your seat for an ancient play. There are good views towards the sea from its vaulted upper walkway. The decorative friezes of theatrical muse masks that once framed the stage now lie scattered across the site.

The River Necropolis
A less-visited group of tombs can be found to the right of the theatre, a 10-minute walk through farmland from the main road.

Known as the River Necropolis because it faces the river (usually dried up in summer), the most important tomb here is known as the Painted Tomb. When it was first discovered by explorers in the 1840s, the tomb was covered in bright pigment, but this has since disappeared. Even so, the reliefs depicting a Lycian family group are still impressive.

Noel Baba Kilisesi (The Church of St Nicholas)

Noel Baba Kilisesi was built in the 8th century to house the body of the saint (which was later lost during a pirate raid in the 11th century).

The church is an excellent example of the Byzantine or Romanesque style. Decorated with beautiful inlaid patterned floors featuring rare and expensive stones and marbles, the church is also worth visiting for its beautiful wall frescoes, the best of which can be seen close to the entrance.

The tomb said to be that of St Nicholas in the southern aisle is actually of a later date, but there is another of the correct date that is now on display in the Archaeological Museum in Antalya (see page 70).

HOW PIOUS ST NICHOLAS BECAME JOLLY SANTA CLAUS

Christianity expanded quickly through the region after the 3rd century AD, and in the 4th century Myra became a bishopric. The first man to get the job was a local man, Nicholas, and he was said to have performed a number of miracles during his lifetime, including bringing several children back from the dead. He was made into a saint after his death.

The miracles St Nicholas performed made him the only sensible candidate for Patron Saint of Children and 6 December was chosen as his saint's day. Over the centuries, in northern Europe and later in the United States, this religious St Nicholas gradually evolved into the jovial figure we know today, who wears his beard and robes because of the snowy December weather of the north.

Xanthos

One of the most illustrious cities in the ancient world – it was even mentioned in Homer's *Iliad* – Xanthos has a wonderful setting on a rocky outcrop with grand views down the whole of the wide, fertile Xanthos river valley. The city was capital of Lycia for many centuries and one of its largest and most splendid settlements.

HISTORY

The roots of the city's history are wrapped in the myth surrounding King Iobates, who sent Bellerophon to kill the fire-breathing Chimaera and later shared his kingdom with him. The annals mention Xanthos in

⬥ *Ancient remains at Xanthos are a UNESCO World Heritage Site*

the Persian conquest of the surrounding valley in 540 BC. When they laid siege to the city, all the Xanthian men died defending their city while the women and children committed mass suicide. A second holocaust occurred under Roman rule in 42 BC when General Brutus attacked the city during the Roman civil war. Despite these events, the city prospered well into the Byzantine era and was an important centre for early Christianity.

In the 1840s, British explorer Charles Fellows rediscovered the site and, as was normal for the time, got permission from the Ottoman authorities to cart away the best pieces for the British Museum, including the pride of the collection, the Nereid Monument – an ornate 4th-century BC Ionic temple.

Today the remains are on the UNESCO list of World Heritage Sites.
ⓐ 63 km (40 miles) east of Fethiye, west off Highway 400
🕐 08.00–19.00 May–Oct; 08.00–17.30 Nov–Apr ❶ Admission charge

HIGHLIGHTS

City gateway

This Hellenistic portal is inscribed with the names of the city's patrons, the gods and goddesses Apollo, Artemis and Leto. Close by is a better-preserved monumental arch dedicated to the Emperor Vespasian who ruled the Roman Empire AD 69–79.

The Harpy Tomb

The tomb (the one here is a copy – Fellows took the original) is decorated with pairs of bird-women, assumed to be harpies. In Greek mythology these mythological winged creatures were young and beautiful, but later they were represented as hags with talons who carried sinful people off to the Underworld. Here they are seen carrying off children.

The Lycian Acropolis

There's not much left of the fortified centre of the city. Archaeologists think it was used right through from the Lycian era until well into

the first century AD, so it would have undergone several rebuilding programmes. Look for segments of beautiful Roman and Byzantine mosaics underneath the protective layer of sand.

The Lycian Sarcophagus
When this pillar tomb dating from the 3rd century BC was opened, traces of human remains were discovered. It is thought that the sarcophagus was reused during the early Byzantine period because a later relief depicting funeral rituals was discovered with the bones.

The Roman Acropolis
On the hill behind the ticket office there are some interesting remains, through nothing worth mentioning individually. The remains of a large Byzantine basilica are undergoing excavations, but amongst the long grasses and woodland you can explore an early Byzantine monastery and there are lots of older Roman sarcophagi and Lycian rock tombs dotted around within the protection of some long sections of city wall.

The Roman theatre
Small but perfectly formed, the theatre's *cavea* or seating area is well preserved.

The Xanthian Obelisk
The remains of another tomb pillar that is inscribed with Lycian script and some Greek text that allowed scholars to translate the Lycian alphabet by comparing the two (apparently it tells of a Lycian man and his deeds of bravery that endowed his family with great prestige).

Patara

Ancient Patara used to be a wealthy city and the major port of Lycia until it silted up. It now symbolises one of Turkey's dilemmas: how to make the most of tourist potential while preserving green credentials.
ⓐ 78 km (48 miles) east of Fethiye, south off the 400 ⓒ 07.30–19.00 May–Oct; 08.30–17.00 Nov–Apr ⓘ One admission charge for site and beach

THINGS TO SEE & DO

The ancient site
Patara nestles amongst wild grasses and sand dunes behind Patara beach. It was important in antiquity for its temple to Apollo, and was also a large naval base. Despite recent excavations, the sand has reclaimed a lot of the city. This is truly a place where you can pretend to be Indiana Jones, discovering the wonderful 1st-century AD city gate, a marvellous theatre and vast 2nd-century AD granaries.

The beach
The longest beach in Turkey, Patara is also one of the most unspoilt because it is a protected turtle-nesting site. There is one lone beach bar and a single line of parasols at the eastern end of the 18-km (11-mile) stretch. The turtles nest at night, so it is off limits after dark from May to October, but during the day you can find a stretch of sand to yourself.

Gelemiş
The village of Gelemiş lies around 3 km (2 miles) inland from the beach, just north of the archaeological remains. At one time the site was due to be yet another tourist resort, but protection of the turtles stopped all that. Today, it is a low-key place with a handful of *gözleme* stalls, plus a couple of restaurant/bars and souvenir kiosks. The government still has not decided what it wants to do about development and, from time to time, the police close down unlicensed premises or issue eviction notices.

Ephesus

The largest and most complete ancient city in the eastern
Mediterranean, Ephesus is a must-see site. The exceptionally
well-preserved buildings, with little touches that bring the citizens to
life, allow us to step back in time to the late Roman era, when this was
the capital of Asia Minor. It is a long day trip from the Lycian region, but
well worth the effort.

HISTORY

Founded in the 11th century BC, Ephesus became an important and rich
city because it was the centre of worship for the goddess of fertility,
Artemis. The temple here was one of the Seven Wonders of the Ancient
World and attracted pilgrims from around ancient Greece.

In Roman times, the city was capital of the province with a
population of over 250,000 people. It was a trading and banking city
of immense wealth and was one of the most advanced cities in the
Empire, with both flushing communal latrines and street lighting.

It was an important Christian city with a close association with
St Paul of Tarsus and was populated until the 11th century AD.

The last few hundred years brought serious problems when its port
on the River Cayster began to silt up. Eventually it was cut off from
the sea completely, making trade impossible. The city was then
abandoned.

THINGS TO SEE & DO

The Upper City

A plateau at the top of the hill is the least exciting part of the city.
Around the wide space that was once the Upper Agora, you will be
able to explore the administrative headquarters, a small *odeon* (theatre)
and the remains of a thermal spa. The best part of the upper city is
the view down over the rest of Ephesus. From the small square in front
of the Monument of Memmius, which was erected in homage to the

citizens of the city, you get your most breathtaking view down Curetes Street, one of the most photographed vistas in Turkey.

Beyond the buildings, look out over the flat area where there is a modern airfield. This used to be the port for the ancient city. Take some time to search for the coast in the distance. This is how far the sea has receded since Roman times and shows why the city was doomed. With no way to transport goods overland, the city couldn't function.

Curetes Street

The major arterial route linking the upper city with the port, Curetes Street had shops selling goods from around the empire, along with a number of important temples in between, including the Temple of Hadrian (built *c.* AD 117–38), with its distinctive double archway of fine Corinthian columns and elaborate frieze dedicated to the goddess Tyche.

Slope House

On each side of Curetes Street lie the residential quarters of Ephesus on the terraced hillside, reached by narrow alleyways. These were the houses of the rich, and one three-storey residence, Yamaç Evleri (or Slope House), has undergone a thorough excavation to offer a glimpse of the Roman lifestyle and interior design. The spacious rooms are decorated with incredible original mosaic floors and wall frescoes that were the height of fashion.

❶ Extra admission charge, but it is worth it

Celcus Library

At the bottom of Curetes Street, the library is one of the focal points of the city. Erected in AD 117 as a memorial to Tiberius Julius Celsus by his son, it has a grandiose two-storey façade decorated with fluted columns and statues depicting The Four Virtues: Goodness (Arete), Thought (Ennoia), Knowledge (Episteme) and Wisdom (Sophia). The library once held 12,000 scrolls and was considered a great centre of learning.

Gate of Mazeus and Mithridates

Linking the library and the neighbouring *agora*, the Gate of Mazeus and Mithridates was commissioned by two slaves freed by the Emperor Augustus who went on to become leading citizens of the city. It is built in the style of a triumphal arch.

Baths of Scolastica

The baths were one of the social centres of the city, a place where men got together to do business deals, debate politics or simply gossip. These were built in the 1st century AD in the heart of the city almost opposite the Celcus Library, and you can still see the hot room and cold room.

Theatre

One of the prettiest and most complete Roman theatres, Ephesus theatre is still used during the important Ephesus Festival of Culture and Art each May. During Roman times, 24,000 people would cram the stands to enjoy drama and comedy, but it was also the scene of many of St Paul's Evangelical speeches. He was cornered here by angry Ephesians when he criticised their beloved Artemis, but managed to escape.

Arcadian Way

One of the first Roman streets to get municipal lighting (in the 5th century AD), Arcadian Way led from the theatre to the port. The widest avenue in the city, much is now off limits, but it is possible to stand at the top (in front of the theatre) and look towards what would have been the warehouse district and the waterfront during Roman times.

Marble Way

Linking Curetes Street with Arcadian Way, the short Marble Way has a couple of interesting things to see. Notice how the marble of the road surface has been worn away by the passing of hundreds of thousands of cart wheels. No doubt these carts were heavily laden with goods for market. There is also an advertisement for a brothel etched in a stone of the road, pointing the way to the entrance close by.

Temple of Artemis

A kilometre (½ mile) away from the city is the Temple of Artemis or Artemision, the most important temple to Artemis in the ancient world. A mammoth building, it houses a life-size gold statue to the goddess. It was so impressive that it was known as one of the Seven Wonders of the Ancient World, but today it is a shadow of its former self. The Goths destroyed the site in AD 262 and much of the stone was later recycled – only the main temple platform and a couple of lonely columns remain.

Although the statue has never been found, there are several stone and marble statues of her in the Ephesus Museum at Selçuk (see below).

Ephesus Museum

If you visit the site of Ephesus, you must also visit the Ephesus Museum in the nearby town of Selçuk (Selchuk). This is where the best of the artefacts found at the site are on display.

The museum is not too big and overwhelming and includes the re-creation of a Roman room excavated at the site, complete with furniture and a small domestic shrine. The range of everyday objects on display is impressive, from hairpins to leather sandals. More precious objects include gold filigree jewellery and fine Samian tableware.

Several rooms display monumental statuary and friezes that decorated temples and public buildings, as well as the Hall of the Emperors, where statues and busts of many Roman leaders have been brought together.

ⓐ 129 km (80 miles) north of Marmaris. Agora Çarşısı, Selçuk
🕐 08.30–12.00 & 13.30–19.00 (17.00 winter) ❶ Admission charge

EXCURSIONS

Pamukkale

Pamukkale (Pamuk-alay) means 'cotton castle' in Turkish, and it is a most appropriate name. This huge natural travertine (a type of crystalline rock) fountain is one of the country's most famous attractions and one of its most beautiful and spectacular landscapes. Terraces of shallow limestone pools, the shape of oyster shells, cling to the hillside like a giant-stepped pool against the blue sky. From a distance it looks like piles of raw cotton, a crop that you find in fields all across this part of the country. Close up, the limestone is brilliant white and its edges glitter like diamonds – so bring your sunglasses!

THINGS TO SEE & DO

Hierapolis

The Romans loved natural springs, which they thought could cure various ailments. Hierapolis, the city they built here on top of the plateau next to Pamukkale, was really a giant spa town. Walk down the Cardo, the colonnaded main street to the Gate of Domitian, or explore the necropolis (cemetery), with its collection of more than 1,200 tombs and giant sarcophagi. The **museum** on site displays a range of items found during excavation of the site.

❶ Extra ticket charge

> ### HOW IT HAPPENS
> The springs that emerge from the top of the hill in Pamukkale are rich in minerals. As the water cascades down the side of the hill, it leaves a microscopic layer of these minerals in any undulation on the ground and in the bowls of the pools. This turns white as it hardens. Over millions of years, these thin layers have built up and in some places at Pamukkale they are metres thick.

◒ *The Travertine Cascades at Pamukkale*

Pamukkale thermal baths

These baths have been open since Roman times and the modern
buildings have been built directly on top of the ancient ones. While you
are bathing, you can sit on fallen Roman columns that lie just under the
surface of the water. The warm springs are said to be good for arthritis,
stress and a long list of other ailments – although most people just

come for the fun of swimming there. Even if you do not want to get wet (extra charge), come and have a look at the pools.

🕐 09.00–20.00

The Travertine Cascades

Several storeys of pure white shallow bowls are filled with azure blue waters shimmering in the sunshine.

ⓐ 240 km (150 miles) northeast of Marmaris 🕐 24 hours (ticket office manned during daylight hours) ❶ Admission fee charged when ticket office manned

> ### SAVING PAMUKKALE
>
> In the early days, there was no protection for Pamukkale's delicate environment. People broke the sides of the pools as they climbed over them and sun oils from swimmers left a residue in the water that discoloured the white limestone. To add to this, several hotels that were built above the cascade began to use water from the spring for their own swimming pools, so it wasn't reaching the limestone pools to repair the damage. By the early 1990s 'cotton castle' was in real danger.
>
> In the mid-1990s, the Turkish authorities instigated an action plan to save the Cascades. The hotels on the plateau have been bulldozed and the waters are being trained over the most damaged sections to make them white once again, a bit like teeth whitening. People have been banned from bathing in or walking on the pools. There is a footpath you can follow as long as you take your shoes off, but it is a bit painful for soft feet! All these changes have made a tremendous difference, and the total area of white limestone has begun to expand again.

▶ *Traditional Turkish souvenirs for sale*

Food & drink

Turkish cuisine is considered to be one of the greatest in the world. Though the days of the great Ottoman banquets are long gone, Turks still make meal times an event.

Freshness is the key to Turkish food – just look at the mountains of seasonal fruit and vegetables on sale in local markets or the seafood on ice at harbourfront restaurants for evidence of this. Dishes are generally cooked in olive oil, and a range of herbs and spices has traditionally been used to add flavour, but these are never overpoweringly strong. For an excellent book on the subject, see *Turkish Cookery* by Sally Mustoe (Saqi Books).

WHEN TO EAT

Turks take a very relaxed approach to meal times. There will always be somewhere open no matter what time you get hungry, though you will find more of a social atmosphere between 12.00 and 14.30 for lunch and between 19.00 and 22.00 for dinner, when other people head out to eat. Only the most formal restaurants close between lunch and dinner, and eateries of all kinds tend to stay open until the last client leaves.

In Turkey, food tends to be served warm rather than hot, which usually means chips arrive soggy not crisp. If you want yours piping hot, tell the waiter when you order.

WHERE TO EAT

Choosing these different styles of eateries depends on your appetite:

Büfe A basic snack bar.

Kahve A Turkish coffee house that does not serve food and is usually a place for men to get together for a game of backgammon or a gossip.

Kebapçı Specialises in grilled meats. They vary from pretty, family-owned establishments with outdoor terraces to small, urban kiosks.

Lokanta A casual, often family-owned restaurant serving a small range of home-cooked dishes. There will probably not be a printed menu, but it is normal to go into the kitchen to see what is being cooked. Point at what you want if the staff do not speak English.

Meyhane A bar- or pub-style place serving *meze* with drinks. Traditionally these have been for males only, but in tourist areas women will also be welcomed.

Pastane Turkish patisseries serving cakes and pastries.

Pideci These small snack bars serve Turkish pizza.

Restoran A more formal restaurant than a *lokanta*. A *restoran* will have a printed menu with prices.

WHAT TO EAT
Meze dishes or starters

Turks prefer to eat *meze* style. That is where several small dishes are served at once and shared by everyone around the table. Try eating *meze* style for a truly authentic experience or order these dishes as a starter.

Cold options include *yaprak dolması* (stuffed vine leaves), fresh olives, *imam bayıldı* (slices of aubergine with tomatoes and onions in olive oil) and *cacık* (a refreshing dip of natural yoghurt and cucumber with a hint of mint). Warm meze dishes include *börek* (filo pastry squares filled with cheese and herbs) and *midye dolması* (stuffed mussels).

Because Turks eat *meze* style (see above), you may find that if you order starters and main courses they will both arrive together. To avoid this, order only one course at a time.

Main courses

The most popular form of main course is grilled or barbecued meat, usually lamb, but you will also find some beef. It is grilled as chops or steak but also cubed and skewered for *şiş kebaps*, thinly sliced for *döner kebaps* or minced for *köfte* (meat balls) or *iskender kebap* (minced meat wrapped around a skewer). Meat is always fresh and is generally served cooked through, not pink in the middle or rare.

Fresh fish is plentiful and delicious. You will find it elaborately displayed on ice at restaurant entrances. It is, however, always the most expensive item on the menu. It is sold by weight, so you choose a fish and it will be weighed and priced for you, then cooked to your specifications. If you find the price beyond your budget, you get the chance to change your mind before it is too late.

You will normally find that your main meal comes with bread and salad and either rice or chips.

Snacks

Turkey has excellent pizza (*pide* or *lahmacun*), though it is lighter than the Italian variety and often served rolled up so you can eat it on the go. Equally delicious are *döner kebaps*, slivers of lamb wrapped with salad in pitta bread, and you can find these on almost every street corner. *Gözleme* are pancakes or crepes with sweet or savoury fillings, while *simit* (bread rings sprinkled with sesame seeds) are perfect for stopping those afternoon hunger pangs.

Sweets

Turkish sweets and puddings are world renowned and make no apology for the amount of calories they contain. The most famous, *baklava* – layers of filo pastry soaked in butter, sprinkled with nuts then baked in honey syrup – is a work of art. Milk puddings are also popular, and are often delicious rich rice puddings evoking those you may have enjoyed as a child. *Lokum* or Turkish delight (a jelly sweet traditionally flavoured with rose water, but you will find many fruit flavours today) makes a great accompaniment to Turkish coffee.

If all this really sounds a little over the top, most *lokantas* and *restorans* offer fresh melon or other seasonal fruit as a lighter but equally delicious end to your meal. The sweet toothed will need to head to a specialist café for dessert. These are often very basic establishments with vinyl-topped tables and fluorescent lights, so they do not get points for romantic ambience, but they are full of authentic atmosphere.

TIPPING

Most *restoran* will add 10–15 per cent to your bill, but you should still leave a little something for the waiter. *Lokantas* will normally not add service to the bill but it is customary to leave 10–15 per cent. Leave small change on the table at bars and coffee houses.

International food

More and more 'international' food has become available in Turkey. This includes all-day English breakfasts if that is what you want, as well as other familiar items like pizzas and burgers. If you want to splash out, the large, upmarket hotels will have formal and expensive restaurants serving 'continental' menus with silver service.

Drinks

The usual array of fizzy soft drinks and international spirits is readily available, so you will certainly find something familiar during your trip. But why not try a particularly Turkish beverage? *Kahve*, or Turkish coffee, is strong but never harsh and served in small cups. Take it *sade* (no sugar), *az şekerli* (a little sugar) or *çok şekerli* (sweet), but never try to empty the cup because there are grounds in the bottom. *Çay* (tea) is served weak without milk in tulip-shaped glasses. Apple tea is a refreshing alternative. Another delicious non-alcoholic drink is *ayran*, a refreshing natural-yoghurt drink. Bottled water is also readily available (don't drink water from the tap).

Turkey produces some excellent wine. Look for the trade names Doluca and Kavaklıdere for quality and reliability. It also brews a good, clean-tasting Pilsen-type beer under the brand name Efes, but for something more potent try *rakı*, an anis-based spirit that is diluted with water. It is taken as both a before- or after-dinner drink, but, at a strength of 40 per cent, should always be taken in moderation.

Menu decoder

A FEW BASIC WORDS

Alabalık Freshwater trout

Aşure Sweet 'soup' of fruits, nuts, pulses and bulgar wheat

Balık Fish

Barbunya Red mullet

Beyti Minced kebab in pitta bread

Bonfile Steak

Börek Savoury pastry usually with cheese filling but can be meat

Bülbül yuvası (swallow's nest) Shredded wheat in sugar syrup

Çay Tea

Çöp kebap Finely chopped meat or offal

Dolma Vine leaves stuffed with rice and herbs

Döner kebap Thin slices of grilled lamb sliced from a cone of meat

Ekmek Bread

Fasulye Haricot beans in tomato sauce

Fırında sütlaç Oven-baked rice pudding usually served cold

Gözleme A wafer-thin crepe with sweet or savoury filling

Güllaç Flaky pastry and milk flavoured with nuts and rose water

Güveç Meat and/or vegetable stew, cooked in a clay pot

Hamsi Anchovies

Haydarı Yoghurt dip flavoured with garlic

Imam bayıldı Translated as 'the imam fainted' – a classic Ottoman dish of baked aubergine with tomatoes and onions served cold

İskender kebap Minced meat cooked around a skewer and served in yoghurt or tomato sauce

Istakoz Lobster

Kabak tatlısı Baked squash topped with clotted cream (*kaymak*)

Kahve Turkish coffee

Kalamar Squid

Karides Shrimp

Karışık ızgara Mixed grill of lamb meat

Karnıyarık Aubergines stuffed with minced lamb, currants and pine nuts then baked

Karpuz Watermelon

Kayısı Apricot

Kiraz Cherry

Kuzu Lamb

Lahmacun A wafer-thin pizza topped with tomato sauce and minced lamb

Levrek Sea bass

Maden suyu Mineral water

Mantı Noodle dough ravioli parcels filled with meat

Menemen Stir-fried omelette with hot peppers and vegetables
Mercimek çorbası Lentil soup
Midye Mussel
Pastırma Dry-cured beef served thinly sliced
Pide Small, flat pizzas with a thin topping of minced lamb or cheese
Piliç Roast chicken
Pirzola Lamb chops
Pilav Rice
Piyaz Haricot beans in vinaigrette
Portakal Orange
Salata Salad

Şarap Wine
Sardalya Sardine
Sığır Beef
Şiş kebap Cubes of meat put on a skewer then grilled
Su Water
Süt Milk
Tarama Pink fish-roe paste
Tavuk Boiled chicken
Tel kadayıf Shredded wheat base smothered in honey syrup and chopped nuts
Turşu Pickled vegetables
Tuz Salt
Yayla çorbası Rice soup
Yoğurt çorbası Yoghurt soup

Low tables and carpet-covered benches – a traditional Turkish café

Shopping

There is something for everyone in Lycian Turkey, with a whole range of excellent souvenirs in all price brackets. You will be bombarded with designer rip-offs offering those must-have names at a fraction of the price back home. Stock up on items by your favourite fashion house, but check merchandise carefully, as quality varies from good to terrible.

Leather is also one of the top-ten buys for tourists. You will find a fantastic range of bags, belts and jackets. Again, designer names predominate but you can find traditional styles or have something made just for you.

Turkey is famous for its handicrafts and these include inlaid wooden items like small tables or chess sets, copper pots, rustic ceramics and pottery, onyx or Meerschaum pipes carved from a hard white clay found only in Turkey.

Gold and silver jewellery is also good value as items such as chains and bracelets are priced by weight. You can have things made at small jewellery workshops within a few days. Gold is usually 14-carat quality. Always check for the hallmark on gold and silver items.

The prize souvenir has to be the handmade Turkish carpet. These have been woven for centuries – each region has traditional patterns and colours. The best are made of silk, but most are wool.

Kilims are different to carpets because they have a flat weave rather than a pile. These are just as colourful but generally cheaper and they make great rugs and throws.

BROWSING

Browsing and window-shopping are not things the Turks do. When a shopkeeper sees you looking at his wares, he assumes you have an interest in buying. Obviously, they would rather you buy from them than from the shop next door, so they will put a lot of effort into getting you to stop, look and try.

BARTERING

Bartering or bargaining is a fact of life in Turkey. It is not something that comes naturally to a shopper who is used to fixed prices, but that doesn't mean it is something to be nervous or worried about. If you are in the market to buy an expensive souvenir such as a leather jacket or a Turkish carpet, you will be paying well over the odds if you simply pay what the shopkeeper asks.

There are several tips to make the bartering process more successful and enjoyable.

To start with, act cool about the specific item you want. Look at several items and then perhaps tell the shopkeeper you want to look in other shops to compare goods.

You will be offered a drink – Turkish tea or a soft drink – and it shows that you are more serious about buying if you accept.

Your first offer should be around 50 per cent of what the shop owner asks, then increase your offer little by little. You will probably end up paying around 70 per cent of the original asking price, but early or late in the season it could be more.

If you don't want to pay the price, simply tell the shop owner and walk away. He may call you back with a lower offer. Once you agree a price it is very bad manners to change your mind!

❶ You will get a better price if you pay in cash rather than with a credit card, and better still if you pay in pounds sterling or euros rather than in Turkish Lira.

Children

Turkey is an ideal destination for children. The simple pleasures of guaranteed sunshine, excellent beaches and warm water to play in will keep them happy for hours. Add to this the child-friendly environment, where children are welcomed in restaurants and cafés, and it makes for a very relaxed holiday. Exuberance is not frowned upon here. Turks love children and allow them the freedom to enjoy their childhood.

That said, you will find fewer attractions specifically aimed at children than in many European destinations. There are no children's museums, few 'theme' parks and no games arcades. But the jet skiing and water rides make up for that, as well as the chance to spot a wild dolphin or turtle during a boat trip.

TIPS FOR A CHILD-FRIENDLY TRIP

Turkish excursions can be heavy on history, and even the most enthusiastic adults can tire of this. Pace the sightseeing so you can alternate days of gazing at ancient buildings and tramping ancient streets with days by the pool or on the beach.

An afternoon siesta will help young children stay up late with the Turkish kids (who are often still playing in town squares until midnight). Early afternoon is also a good time to hide from the sun (see opposite).

CHOOSING RESORTS

You will need to think carefully about your Lycian resort if you have beach-loving children. The eastern section has few sandy bays and these tend to be on the small side. Often one enters the water from cement lidos or directly from the rocks, which doesn't suit young non-swimmers. The good news is that the beaches in the west are some of the best in Turkey, with safe long strands at **Ölüdeniz** (see page 27), **İztuzu** (see page 75) and **Patara** (see page 87). The last two are also turtle-nesting beaches where you may be lucky enough to spot one of these shy creatures just offshore.

● *Boat trip to Kekova*

The **Dalyan boat trip** (see page 74) has something for everyone, and kids love to get covered in the sticky mud towards the end of the afternoon. The **Kekova boat trip** (see page 76) also offers the chance to swim and snorkel in crystal-clear water while gazing at a sunken Roman town.

TAKE CARE IN THE SUN

The Turkish sun is very hot and can damage young skin easily. Always ensure children wear a high-factor sun cream. Reapply this regularly, especially after they have been in the water.

Limit the time children spend in the sun, especially from noon through the early afternoon when it is at its strongest. Make sure they wear a hat and always carry a lightweight but long-sleeved garment for them in case shoulders and arms need covering up.

Keep children well hydrated – they may not complain of feeling thirsty but will need lots of liquid to keep them well.

Sports & activities

WALKING & HIKING

The Lycian coast is home to Turkey's most famous footpath, the 509-km (316-mile) Lycian Way, which begins at Fethiye and mirrors the coastline until it reaches Antalya on the Mediterranean coast. Of course, you don't need to attempt the whole walk to sample some of its delights. The easier sections lie in the west, but the best are the mountain sections in the east offering dramatic views down to the sea. The Turkish Tourist Board has produced a booklet about the route, available from tourist offices along the coast.
Ⓦ www.trekkingturkey.com

If you fancy something more modest in scale, there is a wonderful short walk from **Ölüdeniz** over the hills to **Kayaköy** (see pages 25 and 32).

WATERSPORTS

If you want watersports, choose one of the resorts in the west of the region (**Ölüdeniz**, **Marmaris** or **Çalış**) rather than in the east (**Kalkan** or **Kaş**) as the west has the best beaches. From jet skiing to banana boat rides, there is something for all the family.

SCUBA DIVING

The warm, clear waters around the Turkish coast make for great diving, but because of the wealth of ancient remains lying in the coastal shallows, many locations remain off limits and divers must be accompanied by a registered Turkish guide or dive master. If you are already qualified, bring your certification with you in order to book a guide.

If you want to learn to dive, most large resorts have schools accredited by the Professional Association of Diving Instructors (PADI), where you can be assured of good-quality training. Many schools also offer taster sessions for people who have never dived before. After a little instruction, you will be allowed to do a dive under strict supervision – this is a great introduction to the sport.

YACHTING

Getting out onto the water is a wonderful way to tour Lycian Turkey, and a boat-based rather than hotel-based package holiday is a popular and easy option. British holiday companies offer several different routes for one- or two-week stays. See **Sunsail** (Ⓦ www.sunsail.co.uk) or **Yachting Turkey** (Ⓦ www.yachtingturkey.com).

BOAT TRIPS

A huge flotilla of boats, including *gülets* (traditional wooden boats), offer day trips and these are good value for money, with lunch and drinks included. It could be to a remote beach or a historic site, but all offer delightful panoramic views of the Turkish coastline and a chance to spot a dolphin or turtle. The most popular are the **Dalyan boat trip** (see page 74) and the **Kekova boat trip** (see page 76). It pays to do a little research and price comparison. Check out what is included in the price before deciding.

ⓘ Tickets usually need to be booked the day before

WINDSURFING

Most resorts on the western side of the Lycian coast have small schools offering lessons and board rentals. The gentler winds certainly suit the beginner and the improver. Kite surfing is a sport that is growing in popularity.

PARAGLIDING

Tandem jumps (with a qualified paraglider) from the peaks above **Kaş** and **Ölüdeniz** offer fantastic long-range views of the coast and a great adrenalin rush (see page 60)!

Festivals & events

Turkey's festivals and events reflect its fascinating and unique society.
A secular republic, it is very proud of its fight for independence, marking
the major events with great solemnity. However, over 90 per cent of its
population are Muslim, so they also celebrate the main Islamic festivals,
especially in the countryside. On top of this, Turkey holds a whole host of
sporting competitions and folk festivals.

CIVIL CELEBRATIONS

23 April National Sovereignty and Children's Day celebrates the
establishment of the first Grand National Assembly in 1920, which
saw the end of the Ottoman Empire.

19 May Atatürk Day and Youth and Sports Day marks the beginning of
the Turkish War of Independence in 1919, when Atatürk rallied the country
to fight the forces who had divided Turkish territory after World War I.

30 August Victory Day celebrates the success of Turkish forces over the
Greek army in 1922.

29 October Republic Day marks the date when the present Turkish
Republic was declared in 1923.

10 November Atatürk's Death: although not a holiday, Turks mark
the day of Atatürk's death in a very poignant way. At 09.05 on
10 November, the exact time of his death, the whole country comes
to a standstill for a minute of silent remembrance.

MAJOR MUSLIM CELEBRATIONS

The Muslim calendar runs on a lunar cycle different from that of our
solar Gregorian calendar. These celebrations change date each year.

Ramadan (Ramazan)

For the entire ninth month (30 days) of the Muslim year, Muslims
fast between dawn and dusk. This marks the time when Mohammed
wandered in the desert and Allah revealed the verses of the Koran
to him. Muslims devote Ramazan to prayer, reflection and charity.

Şeker Bayramı (the Sugar Festival)

This three-day festival (pronounced she-ker bay-ramer) celebrates the end of Ramazan. Families party together enjoying traditional foods, particularly sugary foods such as baklava, pastries and lokum.

Kurban Bayramı

This is the festival that commemorates the prophet Abraham offering his son Isaac to Allah or God (when Allah accepted the sacrifice of a sheep instead). It takes place during the tenth month of the Muslim year.

Other Muslim festivals

Other major and minor festivals are not necessarily holidays but are the times for special prayers and family get-togethers, including:

Aşure Günü (*ah-shoo-reh gew-new*) The tenth day of the Islamic lunar month of Muharrem commemorates Adam repenting his sin, the birth of the Prophet Abraham, Jonah's deliverance from the whale and the martyrdom of Islamic hero Hüseyin. Also, Turks celebrate Noah's ark coming to rest on dry land.

Mevlid-i Nebi (*mehv-leed ee neh-bee*) The Prophet Mohammed's birthday is celebrated with mosque illuminations and special foods.

Three other days of celebration where mosques are decorated and lit up are: **Regaib Kandili**, the 'Beginning of the Three Moons'; **Berat Kandili**, the 'Day of Forgiveness'; and **Mirac Kandili**, celebrating the Prophet Mohammed's ascent into heaven.

Circumcision ceremonies

Circumcision is an important milestone in the life of a young Turkish boy and takes place at any time between birth and the age of seven. The child is dressed in new clothes – often a bright satin suit and a light blue headdress, and then paraded around the town visiting family and friends. This was traditionally on horseback but today could be in a parade of cars that travels the streets with horns blaring. After the ceremony there is a big family party.

OTHER MAJOR EVENTS IN THE LYCIAN REGION

April

- On 23 April, **Marmaris Children's Festival** is one of the best places to celebrate Children's Day.

May

- The **International Sailing Festival** in Marmaris sees craft from all around the Mediterranean.

June

- The **Abdal Musa Literary Festival** is held at Elmalı (inland from Kaş).
- The **International Lycian Festival** at Kaş (end June–early July) brings together folk performances from around Turkey.

July

- Early in the month is the **International Festival of the Sea** at Marmaris, and the **Manavgat Tourism Festival**.

October

- Late in the month is an **international *gület* festival** at Bozburun, west of Marmaris.
- Late October or early November is the **international sailing regatta** in Marmaris.

December

- A month of activities at Myra marks the feast of St Nicholas, culminating on 24 December for the **Santa Claus Festival**.

❍ *Finding your way around the Lycian coast*

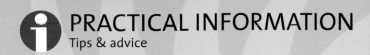

Accommodation

Hotels below are graded by approximate price for a double room (usually including breakfast).

£ = budget   **££** = mid-range   **£££** = expensive

MARMARIS

Liman Hotel £££ Nearly 30 apartments, each with its own kitchen and accommodating up to four people. ⓐ K. Altı Meh. Datça Yolu Sema ⓣ 0252 413 6126

FETHIYE

Atapark ££–£££ Some of the rooms overlook the sea and one of these should be secured if at all possible. There is a pool, sauna, gym and Turkish bath. ⓐ 2 Karagözler ⓣ 0252 612 4081 ⓦ www.atahotels.com

Letoonia Club Hotel £££ Dominating much of the town's peninsula and with six restaurants, nine bars and a plethora of land- and watersports, this is undoubtedly Fethiye's premier resort hotel. ⓐ Paçarız Burnu Mevkii ⓣ 0252 6144966 ⓦ www.letooniaresorts.com

ÖLÜDENIZ

Oba Motel £ Only a short distance from the beach, this is the place to stay if on a tight budget. ⓐ Ölüdeniz ⓣ 0252 617 0158 ⓦ www.obahostel.com

HISARÖNÜ

Montana Pine Resort ££–£££ There is no shortage of places to stay in Hisarönü itself, but Montana Pine is situated outside the town centre (see the website for details of its situation) and benefits from a sense of space and relaxation. Good deals available outside of high season. ⓐ Hisarönü ⓣ 0252 616 7108 ⓦ www.montanapine.com

🔺 *Letoonia Club Hotel, Fethiye*

KAŞ

Hotel Begonvil ££ The best of the middle-range hotels in town, with reasonable facilities and small enough in size to make you feel a personal guest. ⓐ Koza Sokak ⓣ 0242 836 3079
ⓦ www.hotelbegonvil.com

Hotel Club Phellos ££–£££ The smartest place to stay in town and with most of the facilities of more expensive hotels. The half-board deal is worth considering because the evening buffet is a cut above the average (especially for vegetarians). ⓐ Doğruyol Sokak 4 ⓣ 0242 836 1953
ⓦ www.hotelclubphellos.com.tr

Preparing to go

GETTING THERE

Turkey is a popular destination and features in the brochures of all the major package tour operators with a range of hotels and holidays in all price brackets. Prices are highest when demand is high, such as during school holiday periods, when it is wise to book as early as possible, especially if you have children.

If you are more flexible, it will be less busy and cheaper to travel early (May/June) or late in the season (September/October), when last-minute bargains are possible. The internet is the best way to compare prices and facilities whatever time of year you want to travel. If you want to organise your own package you can book a scheduled flight (flexible dates) or charter flight (fixed dates of one or two weeks' duration) and find your own accommodation. Many hotels have their own websites that allow you to make and confirm booking, or use specialist companies such as **Expedia** (Ⓦ www.expedia.co.uk), **Travelocity** (Ⓦ www.travelocity.co.uk) or **Priceline** (Ⓦ www.priceline.co.uk).

You should also check the travel supplements of the weekend newspapers such as the *Sunday Telegraph* and *Sunday Times*. They often carry adverts for inexpensive flights and privately owned villas and apartments to rent.

By air

Most visitors to the Lycian coast arrive via the airport at **Dalaman** in the west of the Lycian region. This caters to charter-holiday companies with flights from many UK airports during the holiday season (April–October).

There are no international scheduled flights into Dalaman. If travelling by scheduled flight, you will need to take a flight into Istanbul and then fly out from there with **Turkish Airlines**, the national airline. It operates several flights a day throughout the year.

The airport has duty-free shops, exchange bureaux, car-rental offices and taxis, but services are limited if you arrive or depart at night.

Many people are aware that air travel emits CO_2, which contributes to climate change. You may be interested in the possibility of lessening the environmental impact of your flight through the charity Climate Care, which offsets your CO_2 by funding environmental projects around the world. Visit Ⓦ www.climatecare.org

TOURISM AUTHORITY

For more information about Turkey before you leave, contact the **Turkish Culture and Tourism Office** (ⓐ 4th Floor, 29–30 St James's Street, London SW1A 1HB ❶ 020 7839 7778 ❻ 020 7925 1388 Ⓦ www.gototurkey.co.uk).

BEFORE YOU LEAVE

Holidays are supposed to be relaxing, so take a little time and plan ahead. You do not need inoculations to travel to Turkey but it would be wise to make sure that your family is up to date with shots like tetanus. It is also worth having a dental check-up before you go.

It is sensible to carry a small first-aid kit with items such as painkillers, treatment for upset stomachs, travel/sea-sickness tablets, plasters, antiseptic ointment and insect repellent. Sun cream is more expensive in Turkey, so buy this before you go. If you take any prescription medication make sure you have enough for the duration of your holiday.

ENTRY FORMALITIES

Documents

The most important documents you will need are tickets and passports. Make sure that passports for all members of the family are up to date. Children already named on a parent's passport can travel without their own passports, but any recent additions to the family or children not on a passport already will need to have their own. These can take up to 28 days to be issued by the passport office, although you can pay more for a quicker service. If your passport has less than three months to run on the date you arrive in Turkey, you need to renew it before you go. For further information on how to renew you passport and for current processing times, get in touch with the **Passport Agency** (☎ 0870 521 0410 ⓦ www.ukpa.gov.uk). When your tickets arrive from the travel agent check that all the names, dates and times are correct.

Keep passports and travel tickets or confirmations in a safe place. If possible, keep photocopies of your passport numbers and ticket information (and traveller's cheques if you take them) separately.

If you are going to hire a car while in Turkey all named drivers need to have their driving licences with them.

MONEY

Consider changing a small amount of currency before you leave, especially if your flight arrives late in the evening or early in the morning. You can do this at a post office, travel agent (allow two or three days for the money to arrive) or at the airport just before you fly. Make sure that your credit and debit cards are up to date before you travel.

Changing money Banks can be found in all major towns. There are plenty of exchange bureaux in resorts. Before you change money check the exchange and commission rates. You will find cashpoints in the larger resorts and there are ATMs (cash machines) at all the airports.

Traveller's cheques These provide the safest way to carry money since they can be replaced if lost or stolen (remember to note down the cheque numbers in the event of needing to have them replaced). However, it is not always easy to find places that will accept them and a steep commission is usually charged.

ATMs These are widespread in the resort areas. You can obtain cash with either your Maestro Card or credit card provided you have a Personal Identification Number (PIN). Your bank or credit card company may charge more for this service.

Credit cards These are becoming more widely accepted in shops and restaurants but not in cheaper *lokantas* and *pide* stalls or in the markets, so do not rely on this as your only method of payment.

❶ You can often pay in pounds rather than in Turkish Lira, so it pays to take some British cash; remember to keep this secure.

Currency The Yeni (New) Turkish Lira or YTL comes in note denominations of 1, 5, 10, 20, 50 and 100 Lira. Each Yeni Lira is made up of 100 Kuruş, which come in coins of 1, 5, 10, 25 and 50 Kuruş. There is also a 1 Lira coin.

CLIMATE

The coastal areas of western Turkey have a Mediterranean climate. This means long, hot dry summers, mild winters with some rain and short, warm springs and autumns.

Average daytime temperatures are: April 20°C (68°F); May 24°C (75°F); June 29°C (84°F); July 31°C (88°F); August 32°C (90°F); September 29°C (84°F); October 24°C (75°F).

In summer you will only need light clothing – breathable and natural fabrics are best – but take lightweight trousers and a long-sleeved shirt to cover your arms and legs in case you get sunburnt.

Early or late in the season take a warmer layer such as a light fleece just in case it gets a bit chilly in the evenings.

BAGGAGE ALLOWANCE

Currently scheduled flights allow 20 kg (44 lb) of checked-in baggage (bags that go into the hold) per passenger, but charter flights have lower limits, as little as 15 kg (33 lb) for clients who have booked at the last minute or bought a flight-only package. Excess baggage costs can be high, so beware. Your tour company will tell you your limit and it will be printed on your ticket. Each passenger is also allowed to carry a small bag (5 kg/11 lb) onto the plane, plus duty-free shopping and items such as laptop computers or cameras.

If you think you may want to take more than this allowance, ask about buying extra baggage capacity before you travel (preferably at the same time as you book your ticket). Many airlines can sell extra capacity to you that will be much less expensive than would be the case if you just turned up at the check-in desk with overweight bags.

If you are going to be travelling with a large item – a pushchair, golf clubs or surf board, for example – let the holiday company know when you make the booking. There may be an extra charge for these.

During your stay

AIRPORTS
There is good road access to the region's airports, but if you are
returning a rental car at the end of your holiday allow plenty of time to
reach the airport and check in for your flight. If your flight departs at
night, the airport will have limited facilities during your wait, so it might
be wise to take drinks and snacks. Also, duty-free shops may not be open
at night.

COMMUNICATIONS
Most resorts have modern public phone boxes that will offer
international direct dialling to the UK. These will operate with major
credit cards or phone cards that can be purchased at press kiosks,
tourist offices and post offices.

Your personal mobile phone should also work, though the cost of
calls is a lot higher than local rates at home. Check this with your service
provider before you leave.

TELEPHONING TURKEY
To call Turkey from the UK, dial 00 90 followed by the city code
(without the initial 0), then the 7-digit number.

TELEPHONING ABROAD
To call an overseas number from Turkey, dial 00 followed by the
country code (UK=44) and the area code (minus the initial 0),
then the rest of the number.

USEFUL TELEPHONE NUMBERS
- **Long-distance operator** 131
- **International reverse charge calls** 115
- **International directory enquiries** 161

Most upmarket and resort hotels will offer international direct dialling that will allow you to phone home from your room, but beware of these, as they often charge a high premium. Ask about rates before making the call.

Post

Post offices have yellow signs with the black letters PTT on them. Most post offices are open government office hours and offer postal and telecommunications services. Most shops selling postcards will also sell stamps for a small price premium. A postcard to Europe or the US costs 0.80 Lira and will take up to a week to arrive.

CUSTOMS

There are no local customs that visitors should be especially aware of because in coastal resort areas Turkish people have become very accustomed to overseas visitors. Turkey, though, is generally a conservative country and excessive behaviour of any kind is frowned upon.

DRESS CODES

Beachwear is best kept to the beach; nude bathing is not acceptable. Restaurants do not have dress codes but smart-casual attire is appropriate for an evening meal in a non-buffet restaurant.

ELECTRICITY

Power is 220 volts, 50 cycles. Plugs are European style with two round pins so you will need an adaptor for your electrical appliances.

EMERGENCY NUMBERS
Fire 110
Police 155
Ambulance 112

EMBASSIES & CONSULATES

The British Embassy ⓐ Şehit Ersan Caddesi 46/A, Çankaya, Ankara
ⓣ 0312 455 3344
Honorary Consul Marmaris c/o Yesil Marmaris Tourism and Yacht
Management Inc ⓐ Barbaros Caddesi 118 (PO Box 8), Marina, 48700
Marmaris ⓣ 0252 412 6486, ext 36 and 39

GETTING AROUND

Car hire

The easiest way to rent a car is through the internet. A good and reliable
Turkish company to use is Decar (ⓦ www.decar.com), with a pick-up at
the airport. An up-to-date map of Turkey's west coast is available from
Roger Lascelles (ⓦ www.rogerlascellesmaps.co.uk).

You will need to leave a deposit and show your driving licence. For all
car rentals, make sure you get a contact telephone number in case you
have mechanical problems. Drivers must be over 21 years of age (some
companies 25 years) and have held a full licence for at least one year.

Driving

In Turkey you drive on the right and overtake on the left (the opposite
of the UK). Speed limits are 50 km/h (31 mph) in urban areas, 90 km/h
(56 mph) on main roads and 120 km/h (75 mph) on motorways and dual
carriageways – unless the signs indicate another limit. Seat belts are
compulsory in front seats and back seats where fitted.

The main coast road and other major roads are generally in good
condition, but small roads vary in quality and some are dirt surface
rather than asphalt.

You will meet all kinds of traffic on the roads, from large, modern
trucks to donkey and carts (and the occasional loose farm animal). You
will need to be on the alert for slower-moving vehicles. Slower traffic will
usually move onto the hard shoulder to allow you to pass.

If Turkish drivers want to cross the traffic, they will often pull over to
the right and let traffic behind them pass before making the turn so
they do not hold everyone up.

When traffic is quieter (at night and on Sundays), Turkish traffic lights are switched to flashing amber. This means that you will need to pay attention because there is a junction or crossroads ahead that is not controlled

Parking is a problem in all the major resorts. Do not park where you see a yellow kerb.

You will find both leaded and unleaded petrol. Not all fuel stations are self-service. A member of staff may come and clean your windscreen. This is at no extra cost, but staff will appreciate a small tip. Some petrol stations do not accept credit cards.

Local buses
The dolmuş is the lifeblood of local transport. These small mini-vans run set routes, leaving the terminus when full and picking up passengers anywhere along the route. There will usually be a service from town to the main beaches and resort hotels. They are cheap and efficient.

Long-distance bus services
All Turkish towns and cities are served by an efficient, modern and cheap bus network that makes an excellent framework for touring the country. The services feature air conditioning, videos (in Turkish, of course), refreshments and programmed stops for meals.

HEALTH, SAFETY & CRIME
Turkey is a safe country and you are very unlikely to find yourself the victim of a serious incident. However, petty crime such as theft can be guarded against with a few simple rules:
- Don't carry large amounts of cash or valuables with you. Take only what you need for the day.
- Leave nothing on show in your car.
- Don't leave valuables unguarded on the beach or at cafés.
- Keep to well-lit streets at night.
- If you are unsure of the route back to your hotel or apartment, take a taxi.

- Be sure to report any stolen credit cards to the credit-card company immediately.
- Report any stolen passport to your nearest embassy or consulate immediately.

Should you require medical help, most hotels will have a doctor on call but you will be charged for the consultation (you can usually claim this back from your holiday insurance policy).

Hospital If you need to stay in hospital there are clean, though limited, facilities in most large towns, smaller clinics in smaller towns. Staff are well trained and most doctors can speak some English. You have to pay for treatment, but depending on circumstances this could be organised directly through your insurance company. If you have travelled on a package holiday with a major tour company, your resort representative will be able to offer advice and help.

***Ezcane* (Pharmacies)** Pharmacists in Turkey are highly qualified and most will speak some English. They will be able to advise you on treatments for complaints such as minor sunburn, upset tummy, insect bites and diarrhoea. Normal opening hours are from 09.00 to 19.00 hours and there will be a duty pharmacist available in every town.

Water Although tap water is clean, only drink bottled or boiled water.

MEDIA

The only English-language newspaper printed in Turkey is the *Turkish Daily News*. The popular English tabloids are widely available in all the leading resorts at a price premium, though they may be a day old. Most upmarket hotels will offer *BBC News 24* as part of their programming. Resort bars will often transmit Premier League matches live, and show English news reports. You will find internet cafés in most resorts.

OPENING HOURS

Opening hours for museums and archaeological sites change all the time. It is probably best not to arrive too early or too late at a site in case the ticket office is closed. For most places in Turkey, as with the rest of the Mediterranean, it is best to avoid arriving during the lunch hours, as most places will shut for a long lunch. Also be aware of seasonal variations – in the off-season, many places will shut entirely or have reduced hours.

Banks 🕐 08.30–12.00 and 13.30–17.00 (Mon–Fri)

Shops 🕐 09.00–19.00 (Mon–Sat); tourist shops daily 09.00–22.00 in the resorts in summer

Government offices 🕐 08.30–12.30 and 13.30–17.30 (Mon–Fri)

State museums 🕐 08.30–17.30 (Tues–Sun); closed for lunch in winter

Archaeological sites 🕐 08.00–18.00 or 19.00 in summer

RELIGION

Turkey is a predominantly Muslim country, though it is one of the most liberal Islamic populations in the world. Alcohol and gambling are allowed. The countryside is generally more conservative than the coastal resorts. If you are travelling away from the coast, or wanting to visit mosques or churches, modest dress would be appropriate and respectful.

SMOKING

The Turkish parliament has passed a ban on smoking in public places, which is due to come into effect in 2010. However, existing partial bans are widely flouted and some anticipate that many people will flout the new law.

TIME DIFFERENCES

Turkey is two hours ahead of Greenwich Mean Time (GMT) throughout the year.

TIPPING

In restaurants, it is advisable to leave 10–15 per cent of the bill, plus some small change for the waiting staff. In cafés and bars, leave a tip of small change. Bell-boys should receive 50 Kuru (see Currency, page 117) per bag, room cleaners in hotels should be left 50 Kuru per day, and shoe guardians in mosques welcome a small tip.

TOILETS

There are few public toilet facilities in Turkey. The best policy is to stop at a café or bar. These are not always of a high standard and some may be the 'hole in the floor' Continental-type toilets. If in a resort, visit the nearest hotel. These facilities should be modern and clean. Always carry a supply of toilet roll or tissue, as few toilets outside the hotels will have a supply. In museums and archaeological sites you may have to pay a small amount for use of the facilities. Keep small change handy for this.

TRAVELLERS WITH DISABILITIES

Turkey is working hard to improve facilities for the disabled but provision is still patchy. Many newly built hotels and public buildings have facilities, but access to archaeological sites and historic buildings is difficult and the lack of curb ramps and controlled street crossings in towns makes movement problematical. If necessary, contact the hotels direct to ensure that they can provide what you need. For further help, contact **Holiday Care International** – they have information about facilities and accessibility in destinations for travellers with disabilities (ⓐ 7th Floor, Sunley House, 4 Bedford Park, Croydon, Surrey CR0 2AP ⓣ 0845 124 9971 ⓦ www.holidaycare.org.uk).

ACKNOWLEDGEMENTS
We would like to thank all the photographers, picture libraries and organisations for the loan of the photographs reproduced in this book, to whom copyright in the photograph belongs:

Letoonia Hotel page 113; Photodisc/SuperStock page 17; Pictures Colour Library pages 105; Sean Sheehan pages 40, 44, 71; Turkish Culture and Tourism Office pages 1, 10, 78, 84, 93; Thomas Cook Tour Operations 5, 9, 13, 24, 31, 36, 38, 42, 51, 53, 57, 59, 81, 95; Wikimedia Commons page 67 (Gérard Janot); Wikimedia Commons page 111 (**Knut Thieme**);

Project editor: Allie Coupe
Layout: Paul Queripel
Proofreader: Jan McCann
Indexer: Marie Lorimer

Send your thoughts to
books@thomascook.com

- Found a beach bar, peaceful stretch of sand or must-see sight that we don't feature?

- Like to tip us off about any information that needs a little updating?

- Want to tell us what you love about this handy little guidebook and more importantly how we can make it even handier?

Then here's your chance to tell all! Send us ideas, discoveries and recommendations today and then look out for your valuable input in the next edition of this title.

Email to the above address or write to:
HotSpots Series Editor, Thomas Cook Publishing, PO Box 227, Coningsby Road, Peterborough PE3 8SB, UK.